# SCALES, INTERVALS, KEYS and TRIADS

## A Self-Instruction Program

By **JOHN CLOUGH,** *The Conservatory of Music, Oberlin College*

W · W · NORTON & COMPANY · INC ·

NEW YORK

*Text and Music Typography by Irwin Rabinowitz*

SBN 393-09625-4

PRINTED IN THE UNITED STATES OF AMERICA

7 8 9 0

## About this book

This book covers four topics underlying the study of music theory — scales, intervals, key signatures, and an introduction to triads. The reader is assumed to know the names of notes in the treble and bass clefs, and the names of keys on the piano keyboard. (A note and key chart appears on page 8 for reference.) Otherwise no special knowledge or musical skill is required.

In recent years B. F. Skinner and other psychologists have brought forth a new technique of instruction based on the psychology of learning. The technique is "programed instruction" and its materials are "programs," of which the present book is an example. In programed instruction the subject matter to be taught is arranged in a series of small steps. At each step the student learns new material by answering carefully sequenced questions or performing tasks. Programs are designed to be used independently by the student, but may be supplemented by classroom presentation of related material. Aside from the saving of teachers' time, some of the advantages of programed learning are: (1) Each student works at his own pace, no faster and no slower. (2) The student is continuously active: he is called upon to apply each new fact or idea in a variety of situations. (3) The student is always made aware of his progress: after each task he finds out immediately whether his work is correct. In these respects programed learning is akin to study with a private tutor.

# To the classroom teacher

This program may be used in high school or college courses in elementary music theory. It is intended to provide a foundation for subsequent work in one of the standard textbooks, and to serve equally well the needs of teachers who prefer not to use a text.

Most students will require 6-12 hours to complete the program. Thus, in some courses it will be convenient to assign completion of the entire program within a prescribed period at the beginning of the course, say two or three weeks. Or it may be assigned in sections, provided that each set is done in its proper turn. (One exception: sets 10 and 11, and the frames in set 12 relating to them, may be deferred until the end of the program, or omitted altogether, if desired.) Following completion of the program a test composed of items similar to those in sets 12 and 24 should be given.

The program has been revised on the basis of trials in classes at the Conservatory of Music, Oberlin College. All sections of the program have been tested by at least one hundred and fifty students; some sections have been tested by more than four hundred students over a period of four years.

It can be reported that this program has done an effective job of teaching its subject matter. However, those who adopt it should be cautioned not to expect miraculous extensions of learning to areas not really covered in the program. For example: a student who has completed the program should know that five sharps is the key signature of B major or G♯ minor. But the ability to identify the key of a given passage in an actual composition is not dealt with in the program, since it ultimately involves a judgment based on aural, not visual facts. The teaching of this skill (not to mention countless others) properly belongs to the classroom teacher.

# To the private teacher

Few private teachers are able to devote sufficient time to basic theory. Many are keenly aware of their students' lack of knowledge of key signatures and other fundamentals. A self-instruction program in theory therefore seems a logical adjunct to private applied study. A good plan might be to assign the student one part of the program at a time and, following his completion of each part, to discuss with him its applications in a piece he is currently studying.

This program was written with high school age and older students in mind, but it may also be undertaken by musically and intellectually gifted students of junior high school age.

# How to use this book

The program is divided into four parts. Each part has several *sets*, and each set contains roughly twenty to fifty *frames*. Frames are numbered within each set and separated from one another by horizontal lines. Each frame presents information, asks a question, gives a statement to be completed, or directs that a certain operation be carried out. Occasionally a single frame may do two or more of these things.

To use the book, cover the left-hand side of page 9 with the masking card. Read frame no. 1 and write your answer in the book. Slide the masking card down just far enough to expose the correct answer to frame no. 1, which lies directly to the left of frame no. 1. Check your answer. Next read frame no. 2, write your answer, slide the card down and check it. The great majority of your answers will be right. When you do answer wrongly, reconsider the question and try to find your mistake before going on.

Continue with frame no. 3 and on to the bottom of page 9. *Do not turn the page yet.* Insert the masking card *under* the left-hand side of page 1; then turn the page. The card will be properly positioned for page 10, which is a right-hand page as the book lies open. After completing page 10, follow the same procedure, setting the masking card in place for page 11 before turning the page. Continue through the book in the same way, doing each right-hand page in order. This arrangement of pages and method of placing the masking card will prevent seeing answers accidentally while turning pages. When you have completed all the right-hand pages through to the back of the book, turn the book upside down and work back through it to the front. Once again, your work will lie on the right-hand pages only.

In writing your answers to the completion questions, observe these conventions: A single blank such as this _____ calls for one word; two blanks _____ _____ call for two words, etc. In a dotted blank ......... fill in one word, or two words, or any number of words you think will properly complete the statement. Short blanks like this ___ are used when the answer is a letter (x, y, z), a sign ($\sharp$, $\flat$, $\natural$, $\times$, $\flat\flat$), a numeral (1, 2, 3, or I, II, III), the name of a note (C, C$\sharp$, C$\flat$), the word *yes* or the word *no*. Short blanks are also used for certain special abbreviations and signs introduced in the book. All other blanks are the same length, that is _____. If your answer is too long for the given blank, simply write your answer near the blank. Many frames require more than one answer, in which case each answer space is numbered: (1) _____, (2) .........., etc.

Close synonyms of the given answer should be considered correct (for example, *little* instead of *small*). To save time in writing answers abbreviations may be improvised (for example, *sm.* for *small*), but *it is essential that answers be written, not merely thought.* Looking ahead at the correct answer without writing is a fatal error. It leads to vague answers, guessing, and, consequently, poor learning. Remember: *you will not be judged or scored on your performance in this book.* Your goal is command of the subject matter *after* completing the book, and the practice of looking ahead lessens your chances of achieving it.

Should you find a set especially difficult, review it before going on to the next set.

When two or more consecutive frames are separated by thin lines instead of heavy lines, the first frame of the group contains instructions or examples which apply to the whole group.

A sheet of music manuscript paper should be kept handy — it may be needed occasionally as scratch paper.

## Acknowledgments

Work on this program was begun as part of an Oberlin College project on programed learning, supported by a Ford Foundation grant. Thanks are due the many musicians and psychologists who offered help and encouragement, in particular my colleagues Robert A. Melcher and Willard F. Warch, who tried out preliminary versions of the material in their classes. Finally, a special word of gratitude to my wife, who solved many vexing problems of spacing and arrangement as she typed the material.

# CONTENTS

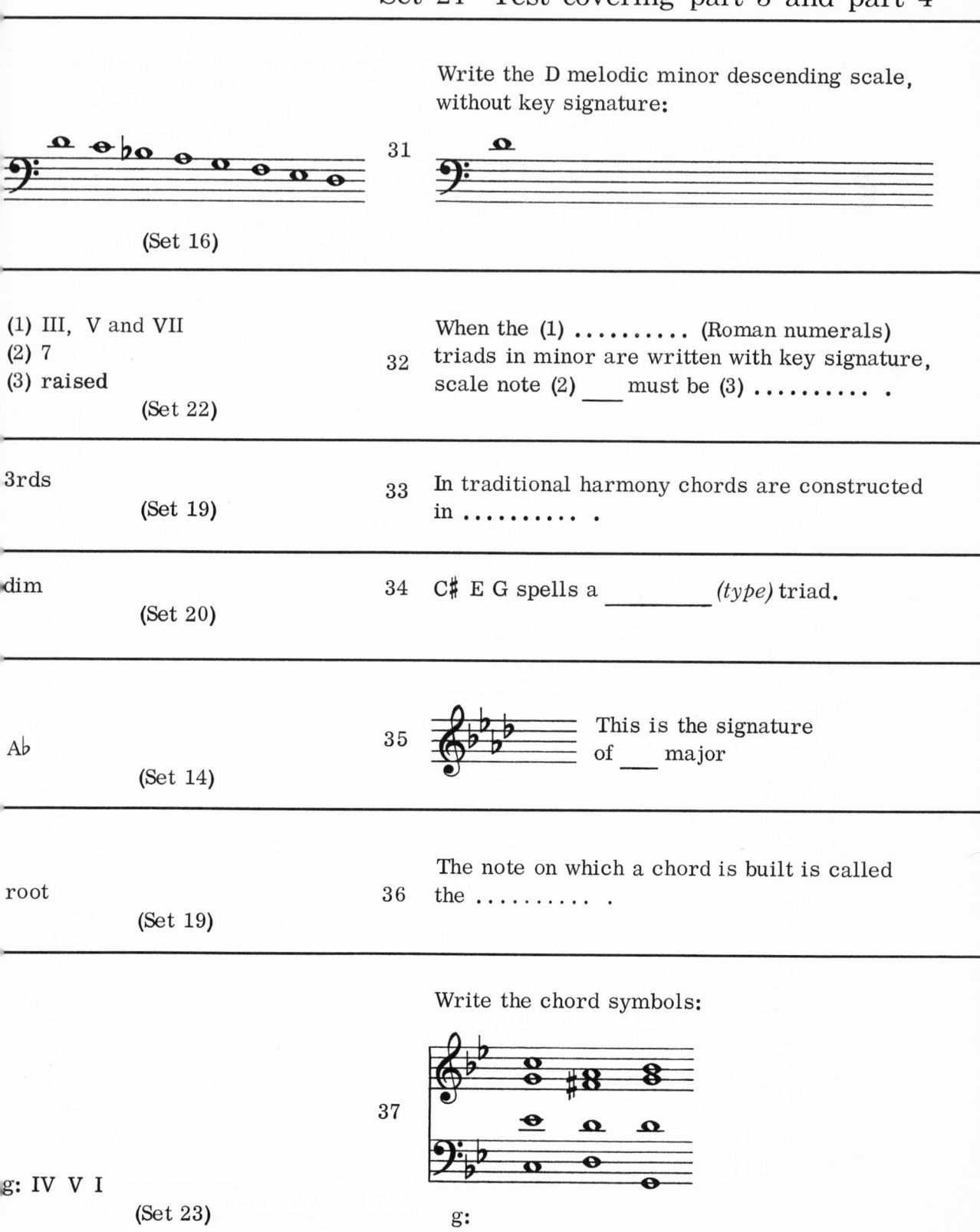

Write the D melodic minor descending scale, without key signature:

31

(Set 16)

(1) III, V and VII
(2) 7
(3) raised
(Set 22)

32    When the (1) ......... (Roman numerals) triads in minor are written with key signature, scale note (2) ___ must be (3) ......... .

3rds
(Set 19)

33    In traditional harmony chords are constructed in ......... .

dim
(Set 20)

34    C♯ E G spells a _____ (type) triad.

A♭
(Set 14)

35    This is the signature of ___ major

root
(Set 19)

36    The note on which a chord is built is called the ......... .

Write the chord symbols:

37

g: IV V I
(Set 23)

g:

The following illustrations, based on diagrams in *Rudiments of Music* by John Castellini, will serve as a guide to note and key names.

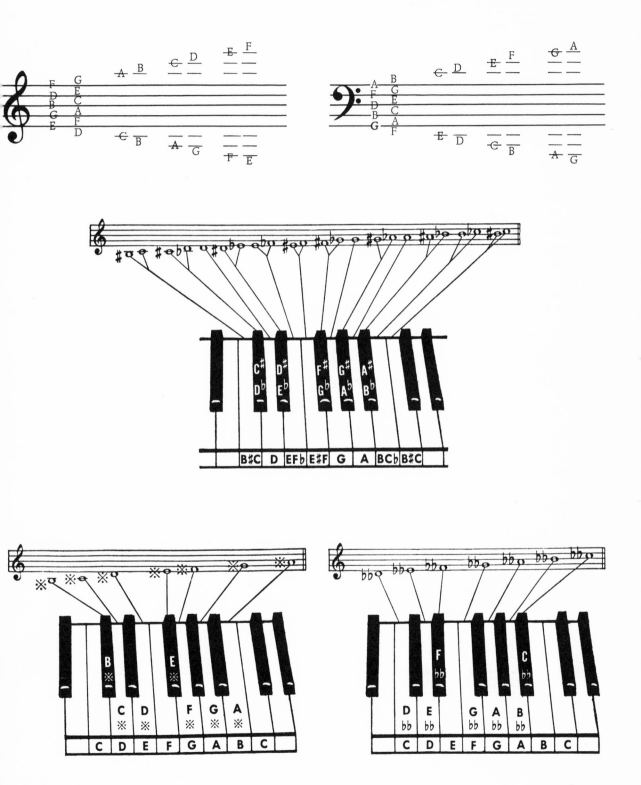

| | | |
|---|---|---|
| Bb melodic minor ascending <br> (Set 16) | 22 | <br><br> This is the ......... scale. |

---

| | | |
|---|---|---|
| root position <br> (Set 23) | 23 | A chord with root in the bass is in .......... . |

---

| | | |
|---|---|---|
| (1) min 3rd <br> (2) lower <br> (Set 18) | 24 | The tonics of two relative keys lie a(n) <br> (1) _____ _____ apart, the minor tonic being the (2) _____ of the two. |

---

| | | |
|---|---|---|
| (1) maj 3rd <br><br> (2) min 3rd <br><br> (3) perf 5th <br> (Set 20) | 25 | In the major triad the third lies a(n) <br> (1) _____ _____ above the root. In the minor triad the third lies a(n) (2)_____ _____ above the root. In both the major and the minor triad the fifth lies a(n) <br> (3)_____ _____ above the root. |

---

| | | |
|---|---|---|
| 2-3, 5-6 and 7-8 <br> (Set 16) | 26 | The harmonic minor scale has DST's at .......... . |

---

| | | |
|---|---|---|
| (1) 6th degree <br> (2) E minor <br> (Sets 21 and 22) | 27 | e: VI means the triad built on the (1) ........ in the key of (2) .......... . |

---

28  Complete the classification of diatonic triads as to structure:

Reference table (Sets 21 and 22):

| | Structural types | | | |
|---|---|---|---|---|
| | maj | min | aug | dim |
| major keys | I IV V | II III VI | | VII |
| minor keys | V VI | I IV | III | II VII |

Answer table:

| | Structural types | | | |
|---|---|---|---|---|
| | maj | min | aug | dim |
| major keys | I | | | |
| minor keys | | I | | |

---

| | | |
|---|---|---|
| 6 sharps <br> (Set 14) | 29 | The signature of F# major is ___ _____ . |

---

| | | |
|---|---|---|
| D  F#  A <br> (Set 22) | 30 | Spell f#: VI: ___ ___ ___ |

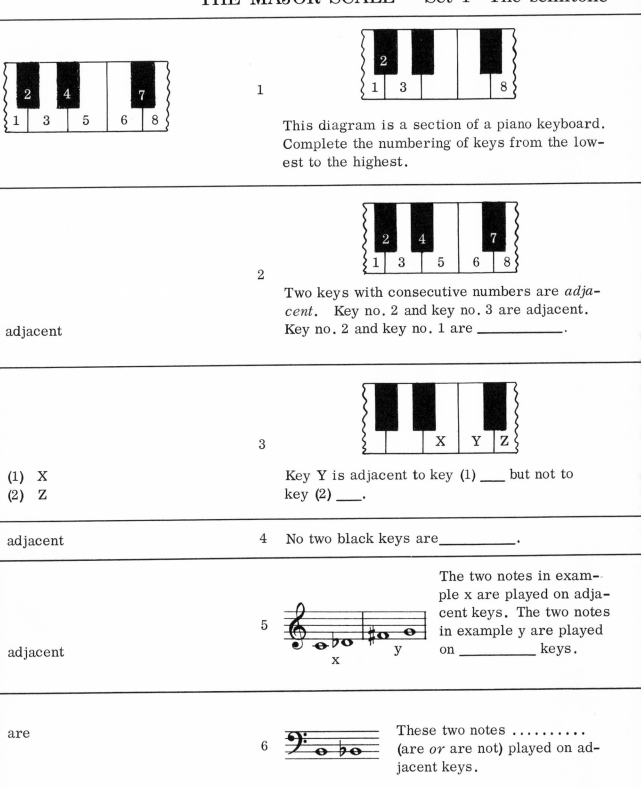

1

This diagram is a section of a piano keyboard. Complete the numbering of keys from the lowest to the highest.

2

Two keys with consecutive numbers are *adjacent*.  Key no. 2 and key no. 3 are adjacent. Key no. 2 and key no. 1 are _____ .

adjacent

3

Key Y is adjacent to key (1) ___ but not to key (2) ___ .

(1)  X
(2)  Z

4    No two black keys are _____ .

adjacent

5

The two notes in example x are played on adjacent keys. The two notes in example y are played on _____ keys.

adjacent

6

These two notes .........
(are *or* are not) played on adjacent keys.

are

| | | |
|---|---|---|
| Bb major<br>    (Set 23) | 14 | This is a ___ _____ *(root and type)* triad. |
| B harmonic minor<br>    (Set 16) | 15 | B C# D E F# G A# B spells a .......... scale. |
| (1) spelling (*or* notes)<br>(2) root (and third and fifth)<br>    (Set 23) | 16 | Chords with the same (1) .......... have the same (2) .........., regardless of octave transpositions and doublings. |
| (1) fifth<br>(2) dim 5th<br>(3) root   (4) aug<br>    (Set 20) | 17 | A diminished triad is so named because the (1) .......... lies a(n) (2) .......... above the (3) .......... . The same sort of statement may be made of a(n) (4) .......... triad. |
| relative<br>    (Set 18) | 18 | Two keys having the same signature are _____ keys. |
| 2–3 and 7–8<br>    (Set 16) | 19 | The melodic minor ascending scale has DST's at .......... . |
| (1) major<br>(2) harmonic minor<br>    (Sets 21 and 22) | 20 | In the major keys diatonic triads are derived from the (1) .......... scale. In the minor keys diatonic triads are derived from the (2) .......... scale. |
| maj, min, dim (and) aug *(any order)*   (Sets 19 and 20) | 21 | There are four structural types of triads: _____, _____, _____ and _____. |

are not

7 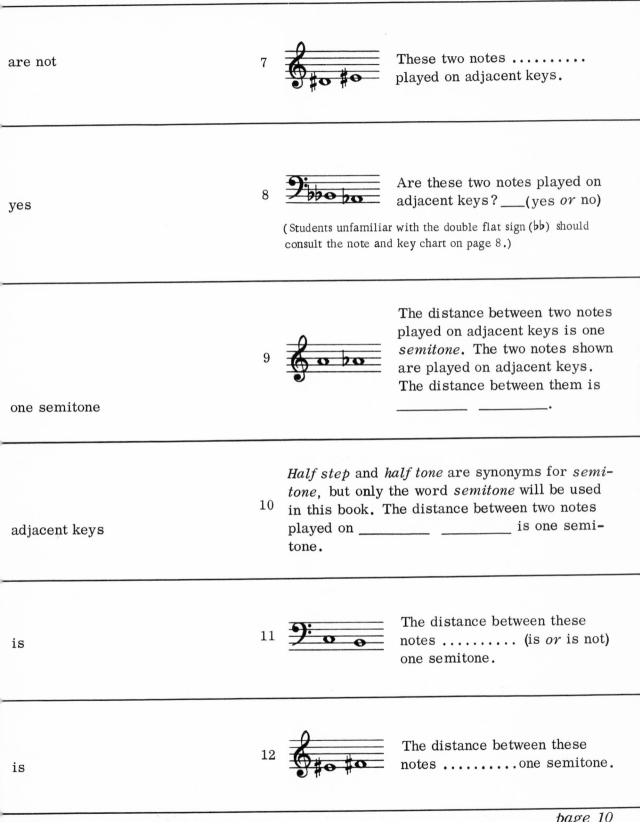 These two notes ......... played on adjacent keys.

yes

8 Are these two notes played on adjacent keys? ___(yes *or* no)

(Students unfamiliar with the double flat sign (♭♭) should consult the note and key chart on page 8.)

9 The distance between two notes played on adjacent keys is one *semitone*. The two notes shown are played on adjacent keys. The distance between them is

one semitone

_____ _____.

10 *Half step* and *half tone* are synonyms for *semitone*, but only the word *semitone* will be used in this book. The distance between two notes played on _____ _____ is one semi-tone.

adjacent keys

is

11 The distance between these notes ......... (is *or* is not) one semitone.

is

12 The distance between these notes .........one semitone.

(Set 20)

6   Write a Gb aug triad:

---

G A Bb C D Eb F# G
(Set 16)

7   Spell a G harmonic minor scale:

G ___ ___ ___ ___ ___ ___ G

---

degree
(Set 21)

8   When, in the key of C, G serves as a chord root, it is called the 5th .......... .

---

(Sets 15 and 17)

9   Write the signature of Ab minor:

---

(1) scale
(2) diatonic
(3) key
(Set 21)

10   Seven different triads may be derived from a
(1) .......... . These are called the
(2) .......... triads in the corresponding
(3) .......... .

---

2-3 and 5-6
(Set 16)

11   The melodic minor descending scale has DST's at .......... .

---

(1) three
(2) 3rds
(Set 19)

12   A triad is a chord of (1) .......... notes built in (2) .......... .

---

E
(Set 17)

13   ___ minor has a signature of one sharp.

---

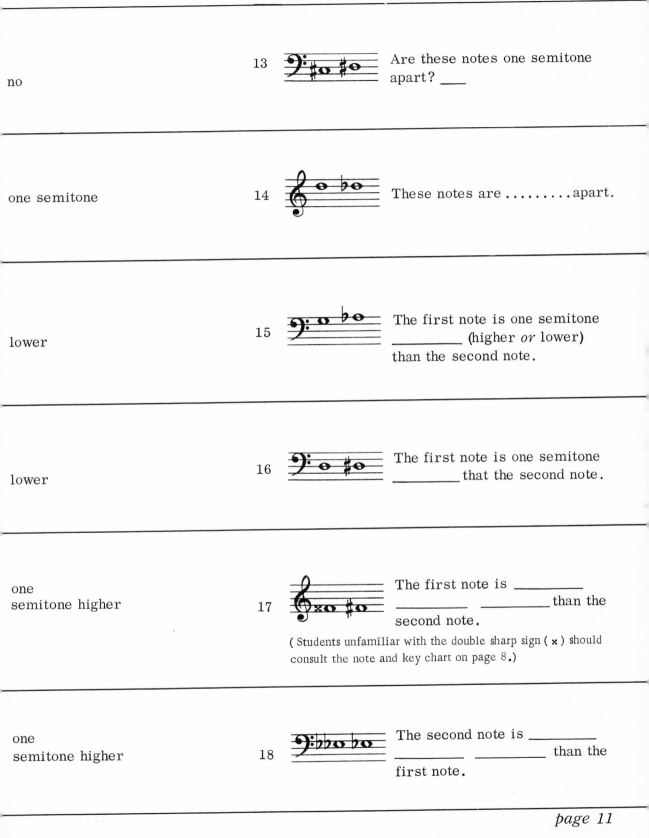

no

13 Are these notes one semitone apart? ___

one semitone

14 These notes are . . . . . . . . apart.

lower

15 The first note is one semitone _____ (higher *or* lower) than the second note.

lower

16 The first note is one semitone _____ that the second note.

one
semitone higher

17 The first note is _____ _____ _____ than the second note.

( Students unfamiliar with the double sharp sign ( ✕ ) should consult the note and key chart on page 8.)

one
semitone higher

18 The second note is _____ _____ _____ than the first note.

This set is a test covering parts 3 and 4. Its purpose is to show what material you need to review, if any. When you miss a question, make a note of the set number given with the answer and review that set after completing the test. Of course, there is always the possibility that your mistake can be traced to weakness in an earlier set than the one mentioned. For example, set 13 (the series of 5ths) underlies sets 14, 15, 17 and 18 (key signatures).

---

(1) maj
(2) min
*(either order)*
      (Set 20)

1

A(n) (1) _____ triad contains two unlike 3rds. So does a(n) (2) _____ triad.

---

(1) minor   (2) major
(3) 2 flats
      (Set 17)

2

G (1) _____ and B♭ (2) _____ both have a signature of (3) __ _____.

---

diatonic
      (Set 21)

3

Roman numerals are used as symbols for _____ triads.

---

melodic (minor)
descending
      (Set 18)

4

Which minor scale(s) do(es) not require accidentals when written with key signature?
. . . . . . . . . .

---

arranging the chord
in 3rds
      (Set 23)

5

When the root of a chord is not obvious it can be found by . . . . . . . . . . .

**19** Write a note which lies one semitone higher than the given note. *(There is more than one correct answer.)*

Write here

**20** Write a note which lies one semitone lower than the given note. *(There is more than one correct answer.)*

one semitone

**21** The distance between these notes is . . . . . . . . . .

is

**22** The same sort of relationship may be stated this way:
Example x is a semitone.
Example y . . . . . . . . .
(is *or* is not) a semitone.

is

**23** This example . . . . . . . . . a semitone.

no

**24** Do these notes form a semitone? ___

Write the chord symbols:

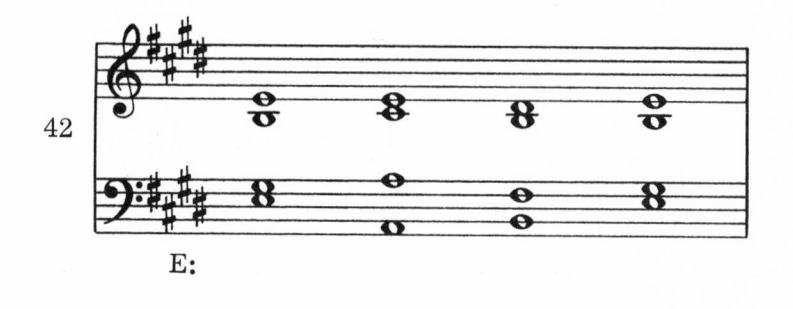

I IV V I     42

E:

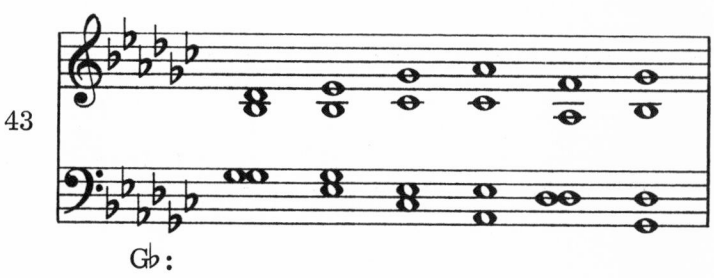

I VI IV II V I     43

Gb:

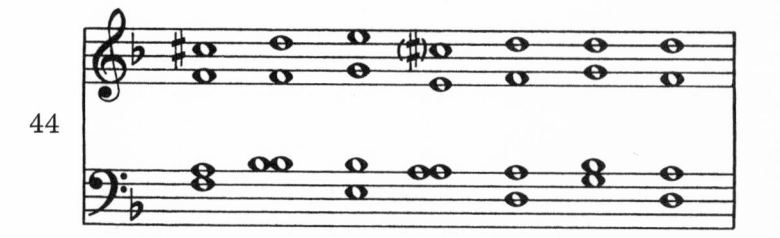

III VI II V I IV I     44

d:

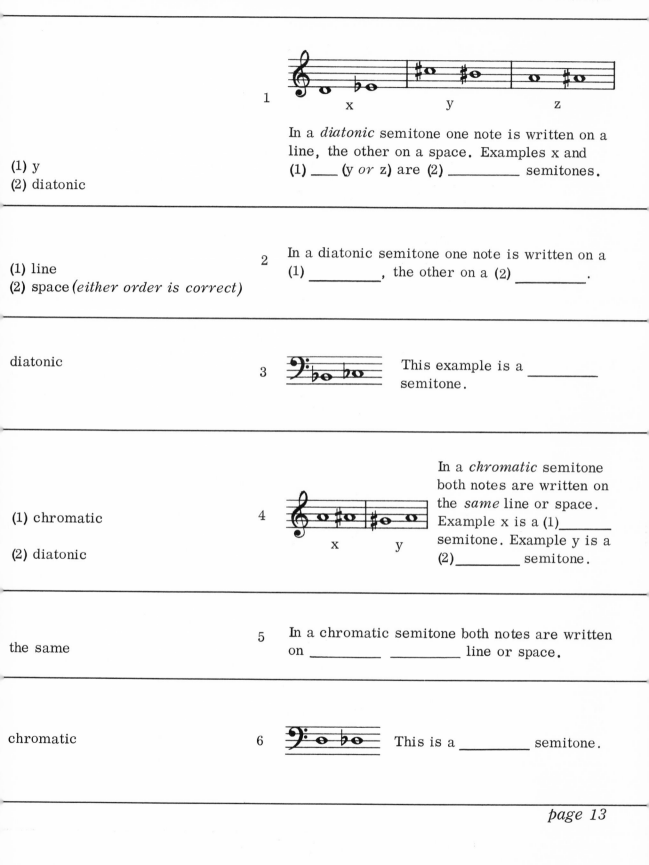

**1**

In a *diatonic* semitone one note is written on a line, the other on a space. Examples x and (1) ___ (y *or* z) are (2) _____ semitones.

(1) y
(2) diatonic

---

**2**

In a diatonic semitone one note is written on a (1) _____, the other on a (2) _____.

(1) line
(2) space *(either order is correct)*

---

**3**

This example is a _____ semitone.

diatonic

---

**4**

In a *chromatic* semitone both notes are written on the *same* line or space. Example x is a (1)_____ semitone. Example y is a (2)_____ semitone.

(1) chromatic

(2) diatonic

---

**5**

In a chromatic semitone both notes are written on _____ _____ line or space.

the same

---

**6**

This is a _____ semitone.

chromatic

---

In the next three frames assume the minor
key corresponding to the signature. Write the
chord symbols:

c: V                                    38

b: III                                  39

g#: II                                  40

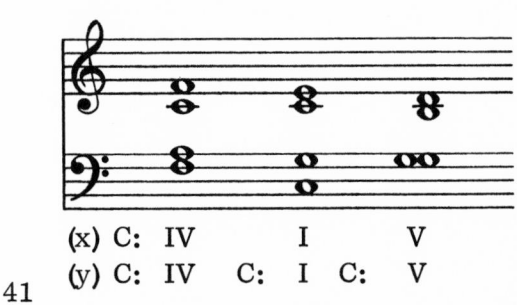

(x) C:  IV          I          V
(y) C:  IV     C:  I    C:  V

41

The key symbol is not repeated for successive
chords in the same key.  This example is
properly analyzed as in ___.  (x *or* y)

x

| | | |
|---|---|---|
| x | 7 | Which example is a diatonic semitone? ___ |

| | | |
|---|---|---|
| (1) chromatic semitone<br><br>(2) diatonic semitone | 8 | Example x is a<br>(1)_____ _____.<br>Example y is a<br>(2)_____ _____. |

| | | |
|---|---|---|
| (1) diatonic semitone<br><br>(2) diatonic semitone | 9 | Example x is a<br>(1)_____ _____.<br>Example y is a<br>(2)_____ _____. |

| | | |
|---|---|---|
| adjacent | 10 | On the piano keyboard two _____ keys form a semitone. |

| | | |
|---|---|---|
| diatonic | 11 | A semitone in which one note is written on a line and the other on a space is a _____ semitone. |

| | | |
|---|---|---|
| chromatic | 12 | A semitone in which both notes are written on the same line or space is a _____ semitone. |

| | | |
|---|---|---|
| | 13 | Write the note which lies a diatonic semitone higher than the given note: |

| | | |
|---|---|---|
| | 14 | Write the note lying a diatonic semitone lower than the given note: |

The remaining frames are exercises in writing symbols for root position triads.  The Roman numeral(s) should be preceded by a key name, making the complete symbol C: I or C: II, not simply I or II.  In the next three frames assume the major key corresponding to the signature.  Write the chord symbol:

35

G: II

F: V          36

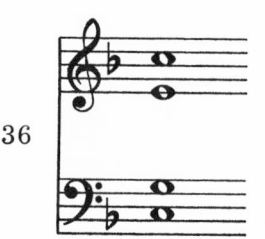

A♭: VI          37

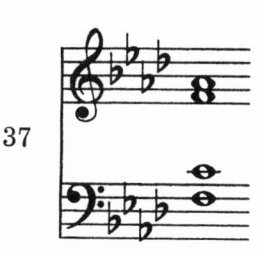

| | | |
|---|---|---|
| | 15 | Add a second note, one chromatic semitone higher than the given note: |
| | 16 | Add a second note, one chromatic semitone lower than the given note: |
| chromatic semitone | 17 | Diatonic semitone will be abbreviated DST. Similarly, _____ _____ will be abbreviated CST. |
| (1) diatonic semitone<br>(2) CST | 18 | The abbreviation for (1)_____ _____ is DST. The abbreviation for chromatic semitone is (2)_____ . |
| DST | 19 | In a _____ (DST *or* CST) one note is on a line, the other on a space. |
| | 20 | Add a second note, one DST higher than the given note: |
| | 21 | Add a second note, one DST lower than the given note: |

To each of these notes add a second note, one DST higher:

22

is not

31

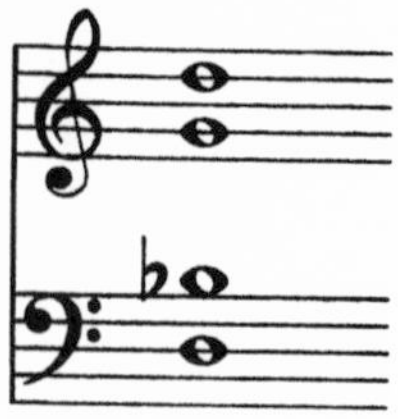

This chord ......... in root position.

Roman

32 _____ numerals are used as symbols for diatonic triads.

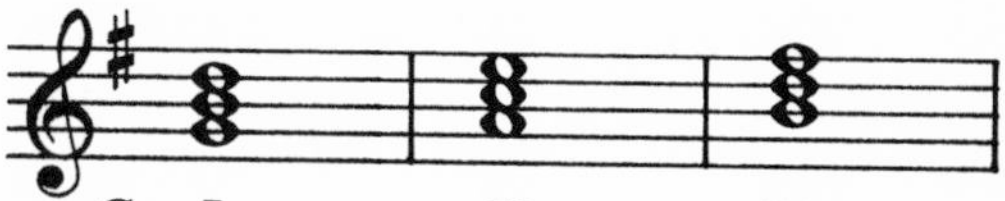

G:   I          II          III

33

root

Up to this point, Roman numerals have been used only for triads with all three notes within the range of a 5th, such as those shown. such triads are, of course, in _____ position.

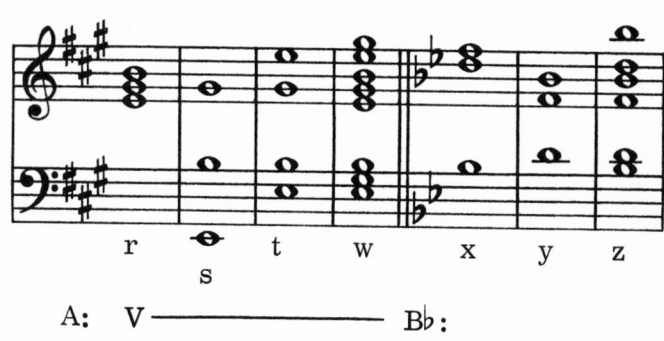

r          t      w      x      y      z
s

A:   V ——————————— B♭ :

34

(1) z
(2) I

The same system of numerals is used for all diatonic triads in root position.  Triads r, s, t and w, all have the symbol A: V.  Triad x and triad (1) ___ both have the symbol B♭: (2) ___ .

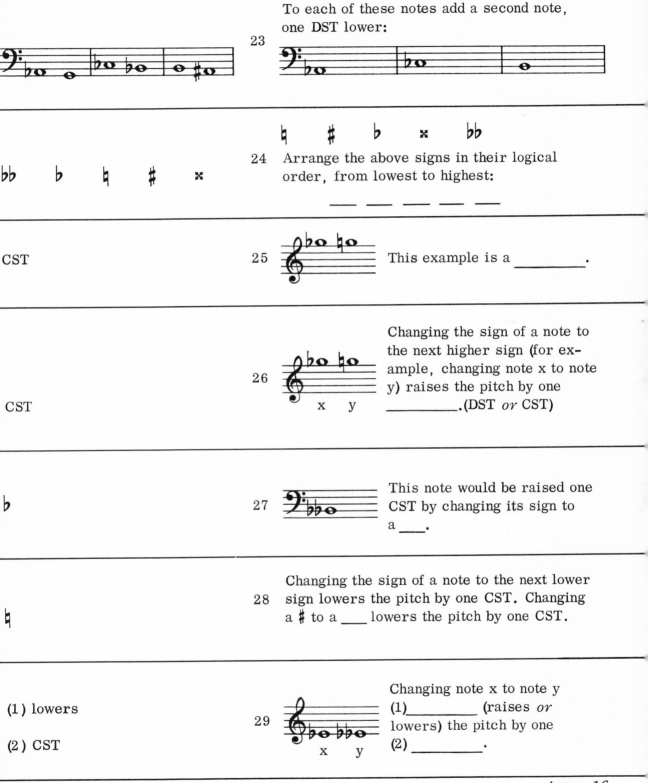

**23** To each of these notes add a second note, one DST lower:

**24** Arrange the above signs in their logical order, from lowest to highest:

— — — — —

CST

**25** This example is a _____ .

CST

**26** Changing the sign of a note to the next higher sign (for example, changing note x to note y) raises the pitch by one _____ .(DST *or* CST)

♭

**27** This note would be raised one CST by changing its sign to a ___ .

♮

**28** Changing the sign of a note to the next lower sign lowers the pitch by one CST. Changing a ♯ to a ___ lowers the pitch by one CST.

(1) lowers

(2) CST

**29** Changing note x to note y (1)_____ (raises *or* lowers) the pitch by one (2)_____ .

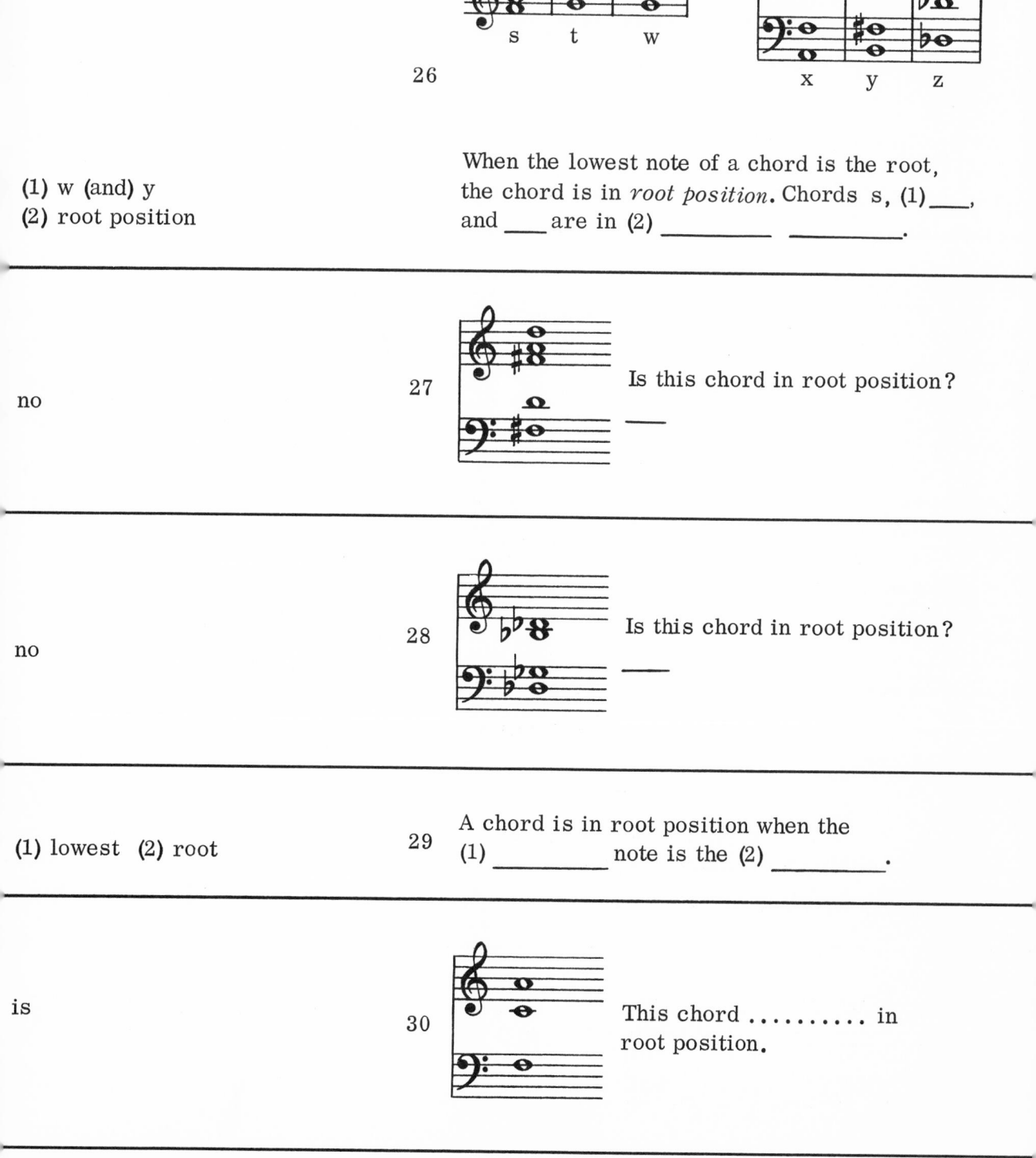

**26**

(1) w (and) y
(2) root position

When the lowest note of a chord is the root, the chord is in *root position*. Chords s, (1)____, and ____ are in (2) _____ _____.

---

no

**27**

Is this chord in root position? ___

---

no

**28**

Is this chord in root position? ___

---

(1) lowest  (2) root

**29**

A chord is in root position when the (1) _____ note is the (2) _____.

---

is

**30**

This chord ......... in root position.

**30** This note would be lowered one CST by changing the sign to a ___.

**31** Add a second note, one CST higher than the given note:

**32** Add a second note, one CST lower than the given note:

**33** To each of these notes add a second note, one CST higher:

**34** To each of these notes add a second note, one CST lower:

**35**
(1) x
(2) y
(3) z
(1) Which example is a DST? ___
(2) Which example is a CST? ___
(3) Which example is neither a DST nor a CST? ___

**36**
(1) neither
(2) CST
(3) DST
(4) neither
Write one of the following labels beneath each pair of notes: DST, CST, neither.
(1)   (2)   (3)   (4)

Give the root and type of each triad:

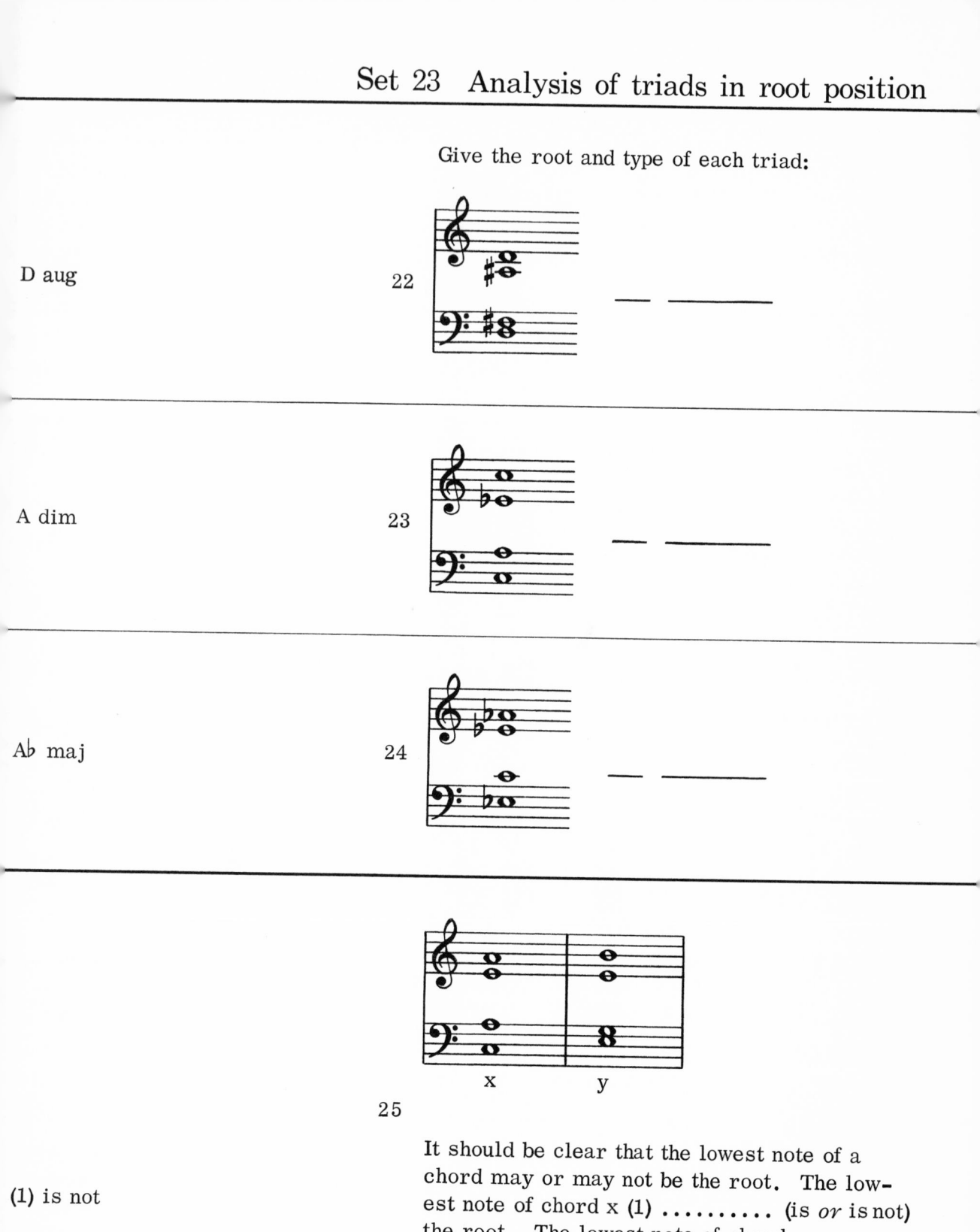

D aug

22 _____ _____

A dim

23 _____ _____

A♭ maj

24 _____ _____

25

x          y

(1) is not

(2) is

It should be clear that the lowest note of a
chord may or may not be the root.  The lowest note of chord x (1) .......... (is *or* is not)
the root.  The lowest note of chord y
(2).......... the root.

# Set 3 The whole tone

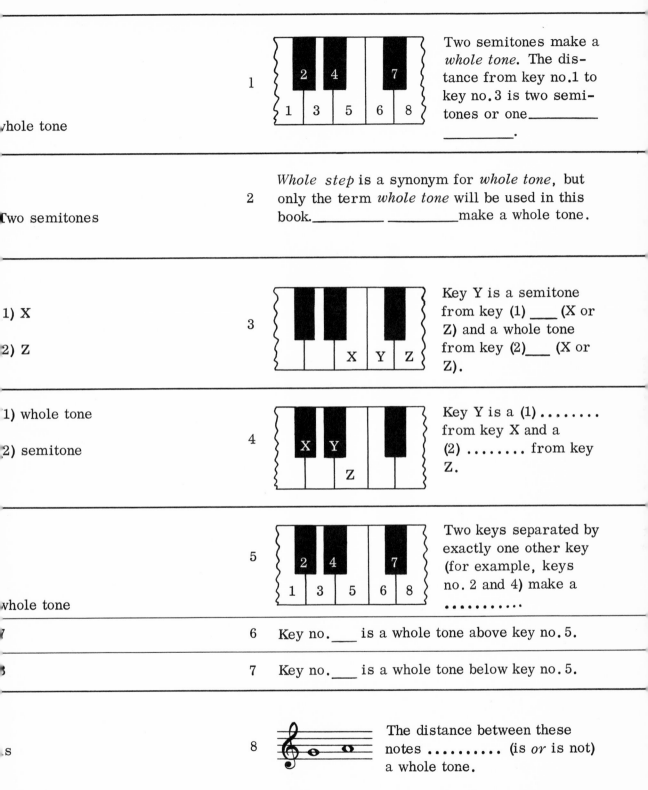

**1**
Two semitones make a *whole tone*. The distance from key no.1 to key no.3 is two semitones or one_____ .

whole tone

**2**
*Whole step* is a synonym for *whole tone*, but only the term *whole tone* will be used in this book._____ _____make a whole tone.

Two semitones

**3**
Key Y is a semitone from key (1) \_\_\_ (X or Z) and a whole tone from key (2)\_\_\_ (X or Z).

1) X

2) Z

**4**
Key Y is a (1) ........ from key X and a (2) ........ from key Z.

1) whole tone

2) semitone

**5**
Two keys separated by exactly one other key (for example, keys no. 2 and 4) make a .........

whole tone

**6** Key no.\_\_\_ is a whole tone above key no.5.

7

**7** Key no.\_\_\_ is a whole tone below key no.5.

3

**8**
The distance between these notes ......... (is *or* is not) a whole tone.

s

**(1)** arranging (the chord) in 3rds
**(2)** lowest

18  When a chord root is not obvious, it may be found by **(1)** .......... .  The root will then be the **(2)** _____ note.

G

19

Octave doubling does not affect the names of chord members.  ___ is the root of all chords shown.

B min

20

The structural type of a triad is not affected by octave transpositions or doublings.  All of these chords are

___  _____

*(root and type)* triads.

A min

21

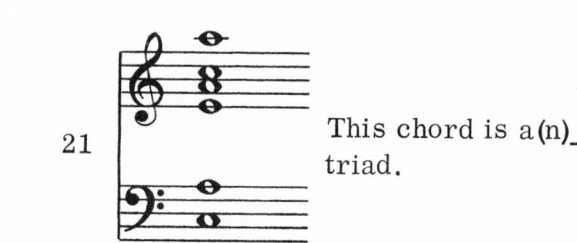

This chord is a(n)___ _____ triad.

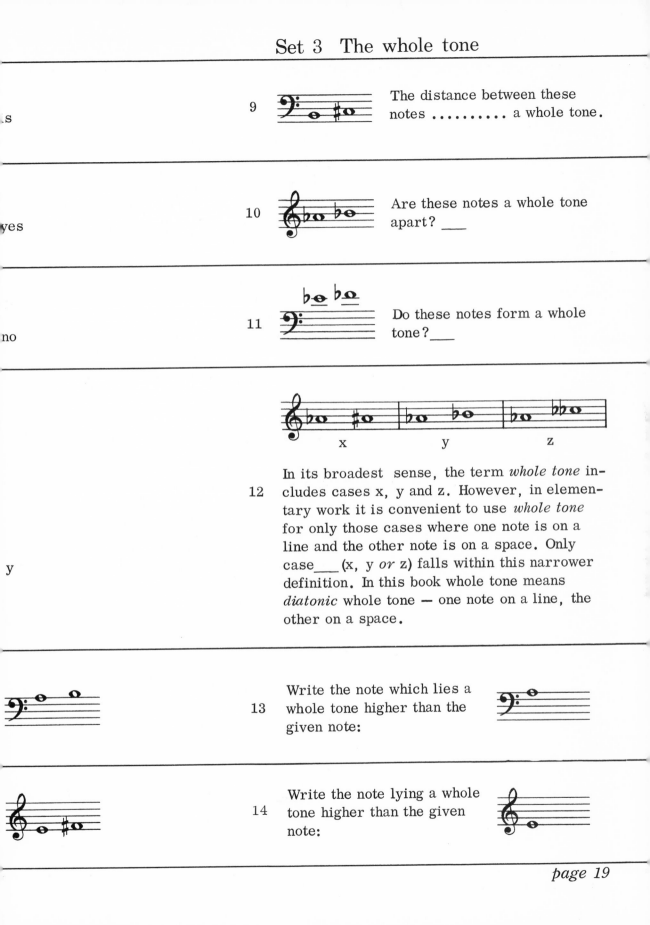

9   The distance between these notes ......... a whole tone.

.s

10   Are these notes a whole tone apart? ___

yes

11   Do these notes form a whole tone?___

no

x          y          z

12   In its broadest sense, the term *whole tone* includes cases x, y and z. However, in elementary work it is convenient to use *whole tone* for only those cases where one note is on a line and the other note is on a space. Only case___ (x, y *or* z) falls within this narrower definition. In this book whole tone means *diatonic* whole tone — one note on a line, the other on a space.

y

13   Write the note which lies a whole tone higher than the given note:

14   Write the note lying a whole tone higher than the given note:

F *(lowest note in*  *)*    13     The root of this chord is ___.

Find the root of each chord:

E    14    ___

D    15    ___

C♯    16    ___

B    17    ___

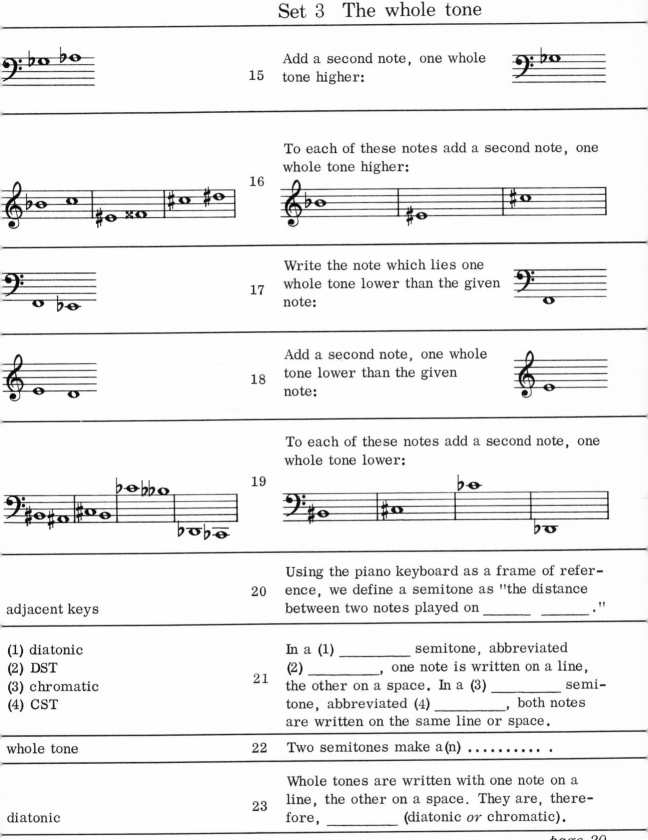

**15** Add a second note, one whole tone higher:

**16** To each of these notes add a second note, one whole tone higher:

**17** Write the note which lies one whole tone lower than the given note:

**18** Add a second note, one whole tone lower than the given note:

**19** To each of these notes add a second note, one whole tone lower:

adjacent keys

**20** Using the piano keyboard as a frame of reference, we define a semitone as "the distance between two notes played on _____ _____ ."

(1) diatonic
(2) DST
(3) chromatic
(4) CST

**21** In a (1) _____ semitone, abbreviated (2) _____, one note is written on a line, the other on a space. In a (3) _____ semitone, abbreviated (4) _____, both notes are written on the same line or space.

whole tone

**22** Two semitones make a(n) .......... .

diatonic

**23** Whole tones are written with one note on a line, the other on a space. They are, therefore, _____ (diatonic *or* chromatic).

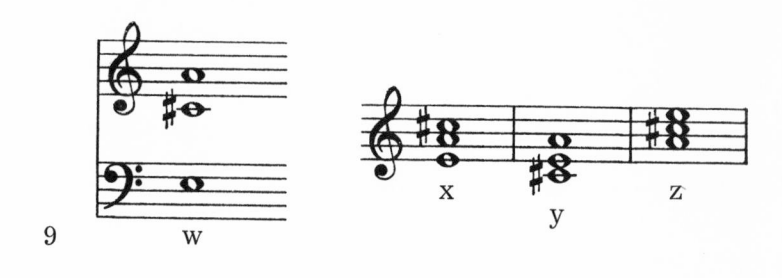

9   w   x   y   z

Chord w may be arranged in 3rds by trying
each note in turn as the lowest note until the
3rds show up.  Chord ___ shows how chord
w may be arranged in 3rds.

z

10

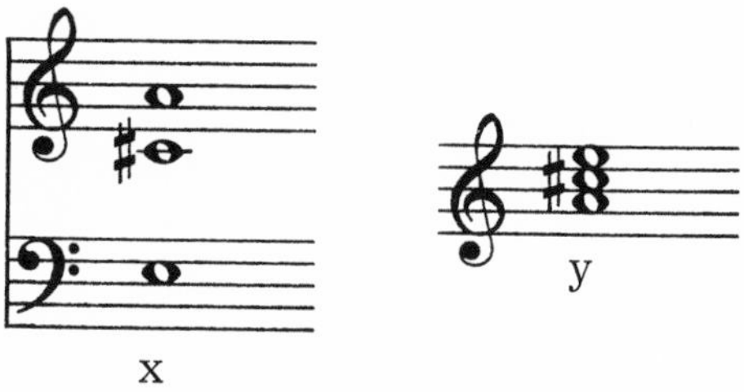

Chord y is an arrangement in 3rds of chord x.
The root of chord x is ___.

A

(1) arranged in 3rds
(2) lowest note

When a chord is (1)_____  _____
11   _____ the (2)_____  _____ is
the root.

Arrange this chord in 3rds. *(Try each note as
the lowest note until the 3rds show up. Do
this mentally, if you wish.)*

12

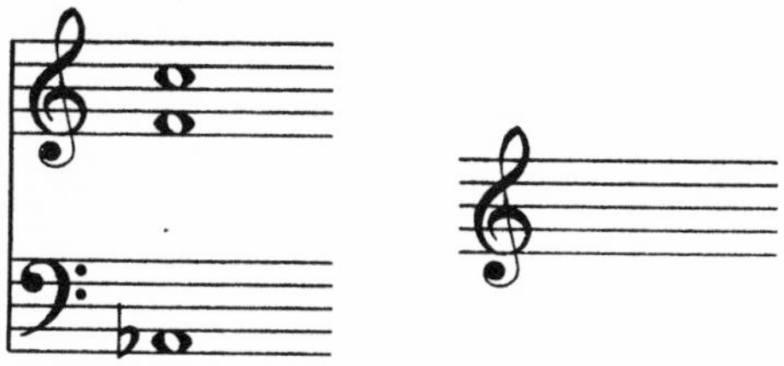

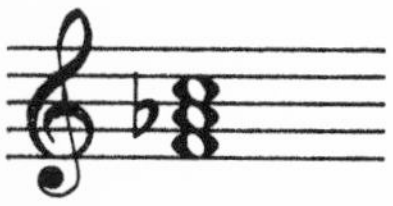

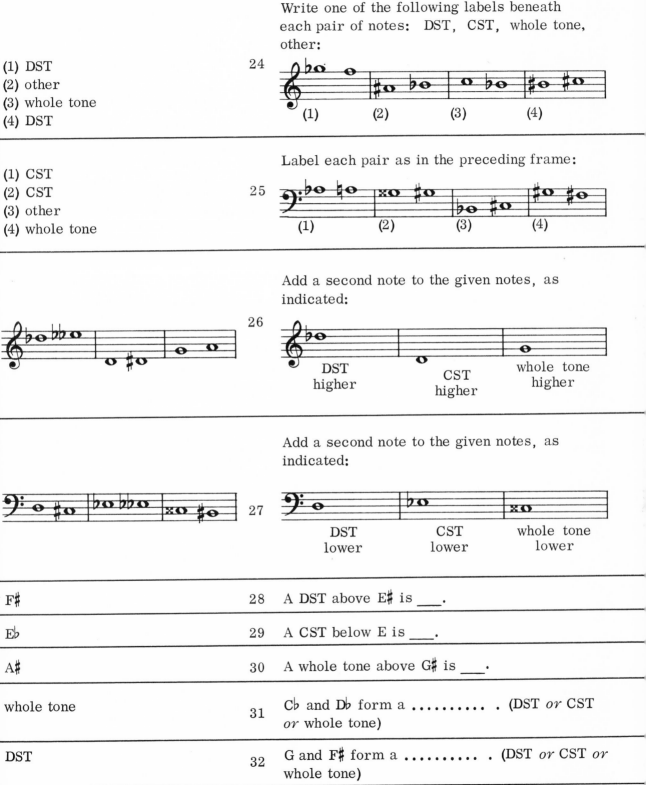

Write one of the following labels beneath each pair of notes:   DST, CST, whole tone, other:

24

(1) DST
(2) other
(3) whole tone
(4) DST

Label each pair as in the preceding frame:

25

(1) CST
(2) CST
(3) other
(4) whole tone

Add a second note to the given notes, as indicated:

26

Add a second note to the given notes, as indicated:

27

28  A DST above E♯ is ___ .

F♯

29  A CST below E is ___ .

E♭

30  A whole tone above G♯ is ___ .

A♯

31  C♭ and D♭ form a .......... . (DST *or* CST *or* whole tone)

whole tone

32  G and F♯ form a .......... . (DST *or* CST *or* whole tone)

DST

C

5   It follows that chords with the same spelling have the same root (and third and fifth). The root of any chord spelled C E G is ___.

(1) spelling
(2) root

6   Chords with the same (1) _____ have the same (2) _____ .

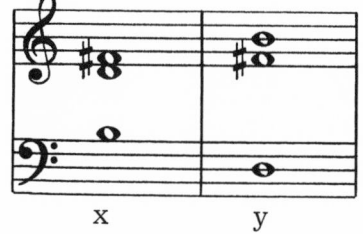

x          y

7

(1) B
(2) B

(3) arranged in 3rds

It is obvious that the root of chord x is (1) ___. Since chords x and y are spelled the same, the root of chord y is also (2) ___, but this might not be obvious if chord x were not present for comparison. It is easier to find the root of chord x than the root of chord y, because chord x is arranged in 3rds and and chord y is not (3) _____ _____ _____ .

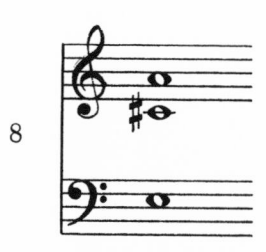

8

no

Is this chord arranged in 3rds? ___

# Set 4  The major scale

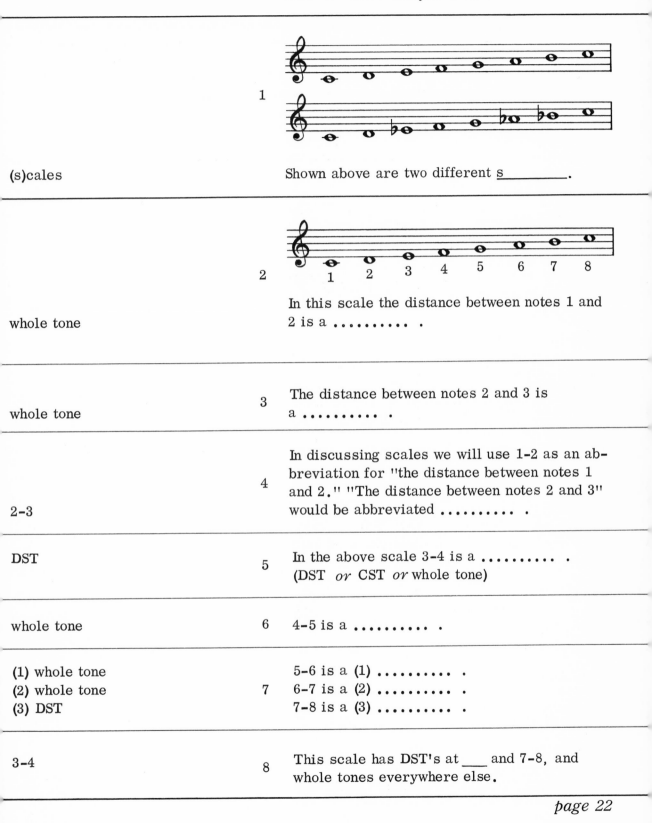

(s)cales

Shown above are two different s_____.

---

whole tone

In this scale the distance between notes 1 and 2 is a . . . . . . . . . . .

---

whole tone

The distance between notes 2 and 3 is a . . . . . . . . . . .

---

2-3

In discussing scales we will use 1-2 as an abbreviation for "the distance between notes 1 and 2." "The distance between notes 2 and 3" would be abbreviated . . . . . . . . . . .

---

DST

In the above scale 3-4 is a . . . . . . . . . . .
(DST *or* CST *or* whole tone)

---

whole tone

4-5 is a . . . . . . . . . . .

---

(1) whole tone
(2) whole tone
(3) DST

5-6 is a (1) . . . . . . . . . . .
6-7 is a (2) . . . . . . . . . . .
7-8 is a (3) . . . . . . . . . . .

---

3-4

This scale has DST's at ___ and 7-8, and whole tones everywhere else.

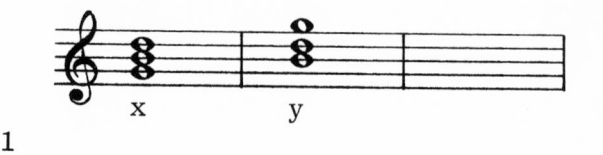

1

If the G in chord x is transposed up an octave, chord y results. Write the chord which re-sults when the D in chord x is transposed down an octave.

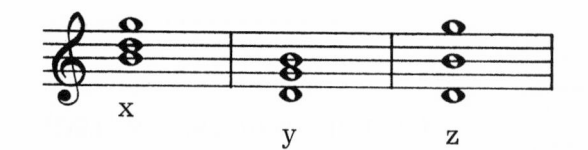

2

Chords do not lose their identity or change their spelling when one or more notes are transposed up or down an octave. Chords x and y are different forms of G B D. Chord z

G B D

is still another form of .......... .

By transposing one or more notes of this chord one or more octaves we can obtain a very large number of chords, a few of which are shown below.

3

(1) G B D

All of these chords are spelled (1) ___ ___. Octave transposition simply results in different chords with the same

(2) spelling (*or* notes)

(2) _____ .

All members of a chord keep their original names — root, third and fifth — regardless of

4  octave transpositions. In all of the chords shown in frame 3, G is the root, B is the

(1) third   (2) fifth

(1) _____ and D is the (2) _____ .

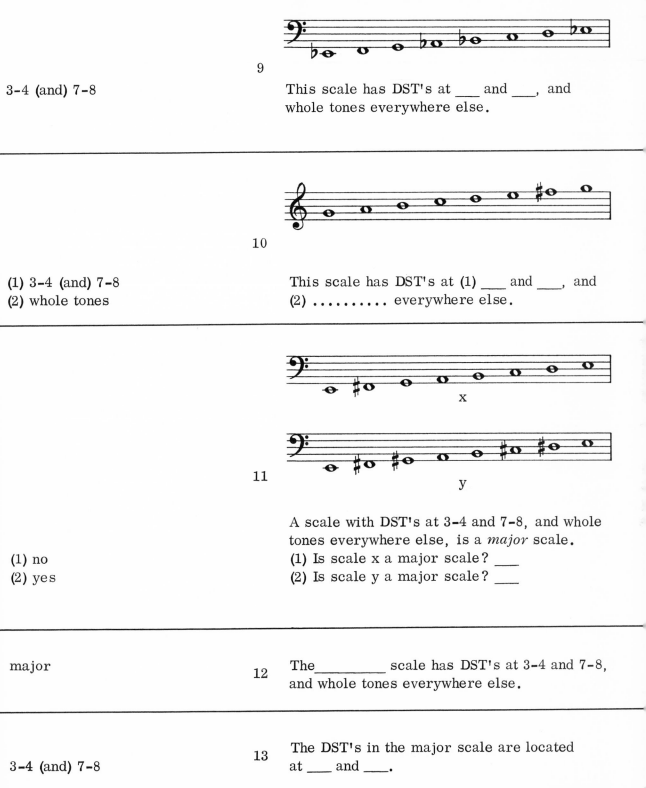

3-4 (and) 7-8

9

This scale has DST's at ___ and ___, and whole tones everywhere else.

(1) 3-4 (and) 7-8
(2) whole tones

10

This scale has DST's at (1) ___ and ___, and (2) ......... everywhere else.

11

x

y

A scale with DST's at 3-4 and 7-8, and whole tones everywhere else, is a *major* scale.
(1) Is scale x a major scale? ___
(2) Is scale y a major scale? ___

(1) no
(2) yes

major

12

The_____ scale has DST's at 3-4 and 7-8, and whole tones everywhere else.

3-4 (and) 7-8

13

The DST's in the major scale are located at ___ and ___.

| | | |
|---|---|---|
| (1) I, IV and V<br>(2) II, III and VI<br>(3) VII | 47 | In any *major* key the major triads are<br>(1) ..........; the minor triads are<br>(2) ..........; and the diminished triad is<br>(3) ___ . |

| | | | |
|---|---|---|---|
| (1) V VI<br>(2) I  IV<br>(3) II  VII<br>(4) III | 48 | List the diatonic triads in the *minor* keys according to structural type:<br><br>major:     (1) ..........<br>minor:     (2) ..........<br>diminished: (3) ..........<br>augmented: (4) .......... | |

| | | |
|---|---|---|
| no<br>*(I is a major triad in the major keys and a minor triad in the minor keys.)* | 49 | Does I have the same structure in the major keys as in the minor keys? ___ |

| | | |
|---|---|---|
| II  no | 50 | Does II have the same structure in the major keys as in the minor keys? ___ |

| | | |
|---|---|---|
| III  no | 51 | Does III? ___ |

| | | |
|---|---|---|
| IV  no | 52 | IV? ___ |

| | | |
|---|---|---|
| V  yes | 53 | V? ___ |

| | | |
|---|---|---|
| VI  no | 54 | VI? ___ |

| | | |
|---|---|---|
| VII  yes | 55 | VII? ___ |

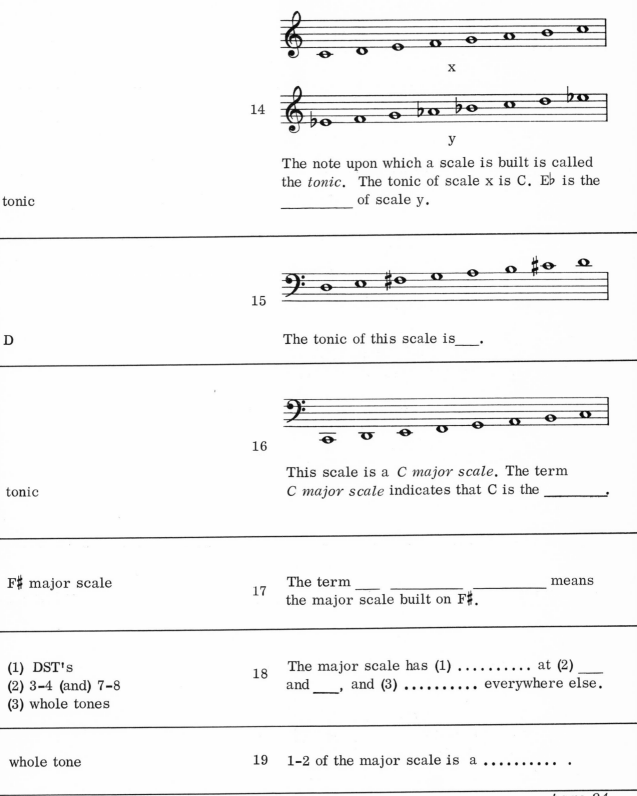

14

The note upon which a scale is built is called the *tonic*. The tonic of scale x is C. E♭ is the _____ of scale y.

tonic

15

The tonic of this scale is___.

D

16

This scale is a *C major scale*. The term *C major scale* indicates that C is the _____ .

tonic

F♯ major scale

17   The term ___ _____ _____ means the major scale built on F♯.

(1) DST's
(2) 3-4 (and) 7-8
(3) whole tones

18   The major scale has (1) .......... at (2) ___ and ___, and (3) .......... everywhere else.

whole tone

19   1-2 of the major scale is a .......... .

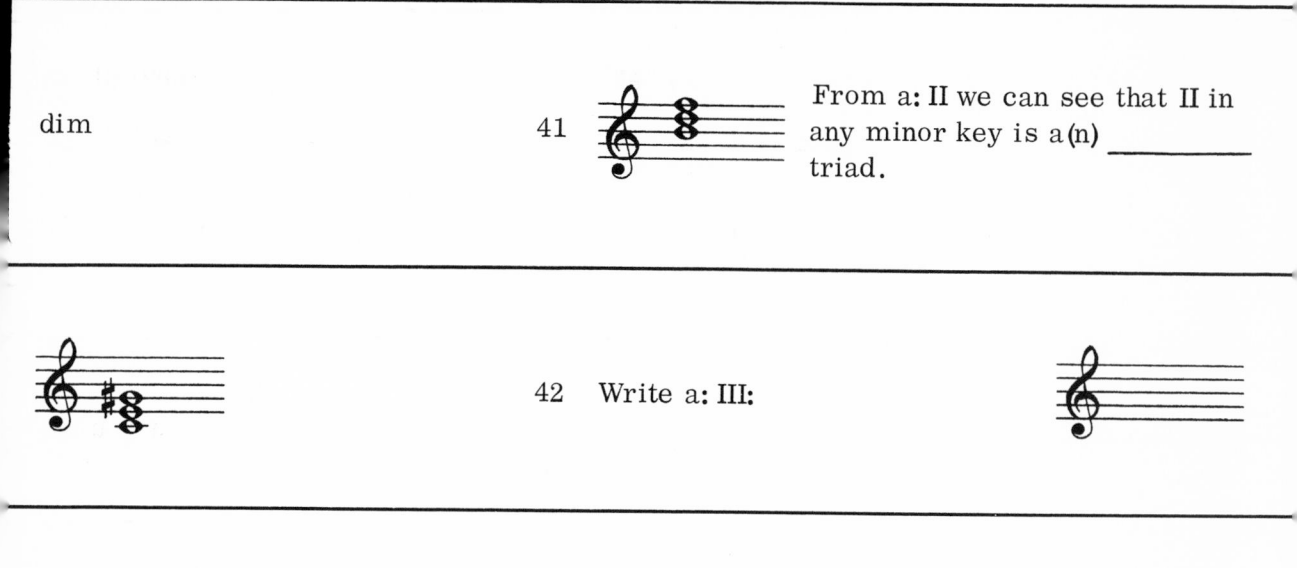

dim

41  From a: II we can see that II in any minor key is a(n) _____ triad.

42  Write a: III:

aug

43  From a: III we can see that III is a(n) _____ triad in any minor key.

Complete the structural description of diatonic triads in minor keys:

|     |     |     |
| --- | --- | --- |
| 44  | I   | min |
|     | II  | dim |
|     | III | aug |
|     | IV  | ____ |
|     | V   | ____ |
|     | VI  | ____ |
|     | VII | ____ |

IV   min
V    maj
VI   maj
VII  dim

one (VII)

45  Of the seven diatonic triads in the *major* keys, how many are dimininished triads? _____

46  Of the seven diatonic triads in the *major* keys, how many are augmented triads? _____

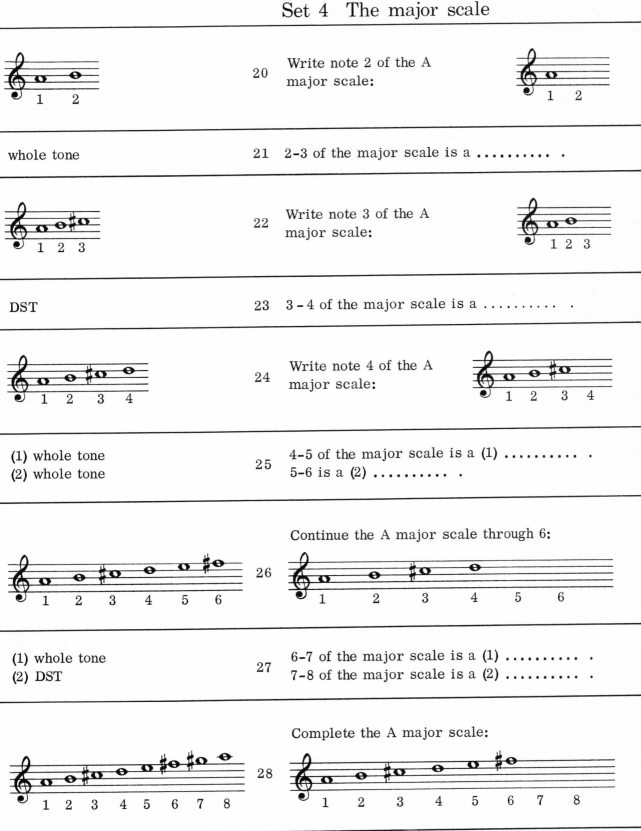

**20** Write note 2 of the A major scale:

whole tone

**21** 2-3 of the major scale is a .......... .

**22** Write note 3 of the A major scale:

DST

**23** 3 - 4 of the major scale is a .......... .

**24** Write note 4 of the A major scale:

(1) whole tone
(2) whole tone

**25** 4-5 of the major scale is a (1) .......... .
5-6 is a (2) .......... .

Continue the A major scale through 6:

**26**

(1) whole tone
(2) DST

**27** 6-7 of the major scale is a (1) .......... .
7-8 of the major scale is a (2) .......... .

Complete the A major scale:

**28**

| | | |
|---|---|---|
| | 35 | Write bb: V, without key signature: |
| | 36 | Write g#: IV, without key signature: |
| D   F   A | 37 | Spell d: I: ___ ___ ___ |
| B   D#   F# | 38 | Spell e: V: ___ ___ ___ |
| min | 39 | A diatonic triad from one major scale has the same structure as the corresponding diatonic triad from another major scale. For example, in any *major* key VI is a(n) _____ triad. |
| (1) min<br>(2) min<br>(3) min | 40 | Similarly, a diatonic triad from one harmonic minor scale has the same structure as its counterpart from any other harmonic minor scale. a: I is a(n) (1) _____ triad. e: I is a(n) (2) _____ triad, etc. In *any* minor key, I is a(n) (3) _____ triad. |

Write the E♭ major scale. (The "½'s" show DST locations.)

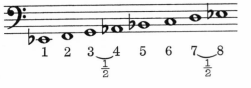

29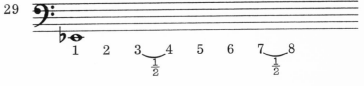

The location of one DST is marked "½." Mark the location of the other one and construct the B major scale:

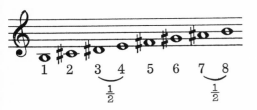

30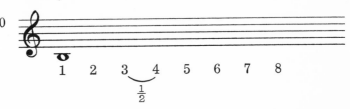

Mark the locations of the DST's and contruct the B♭ major scale:

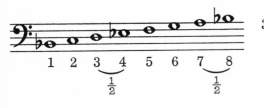

31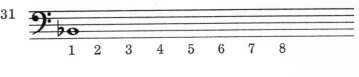

Construct the G major scale. (*Write the note numbers and mark the DST locations first, if you wish.*)

32

Write the G♭ major scale:

33

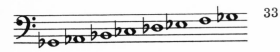

Write the indicated triads with key signature:

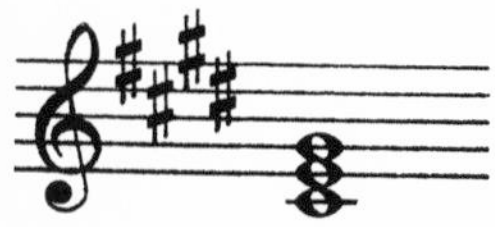

27 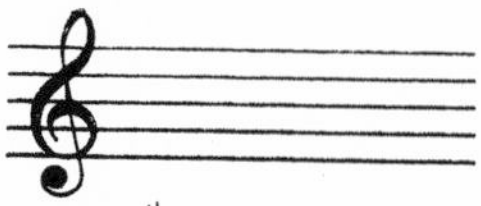    c#:   I

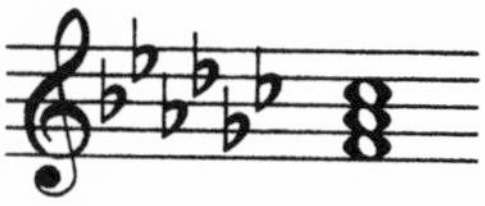

28    eb:   II

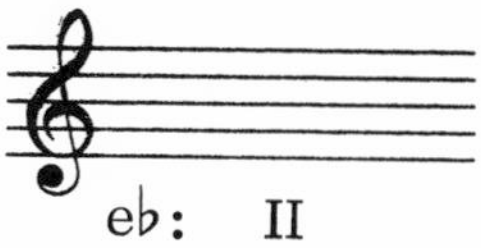

29    ab:   IV

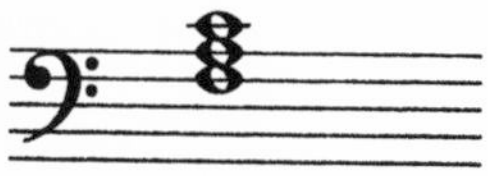

30 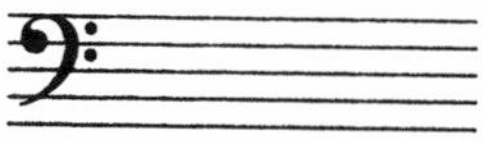    a:   VI

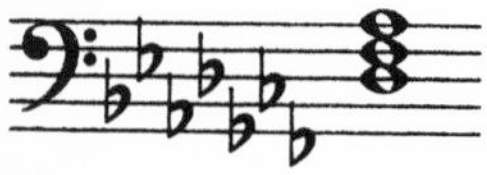

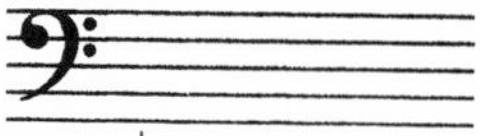

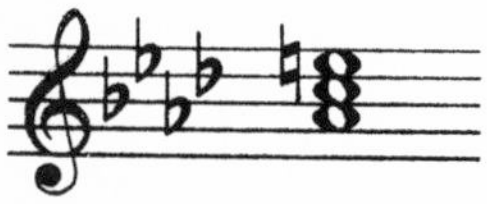

31 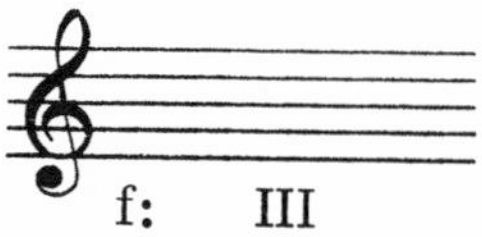    f:   III

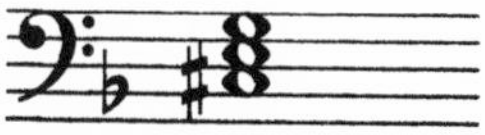

32    d:   VII

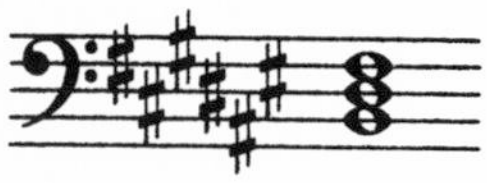

33 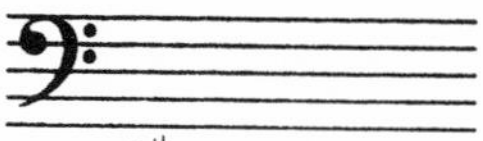    d#:   VI

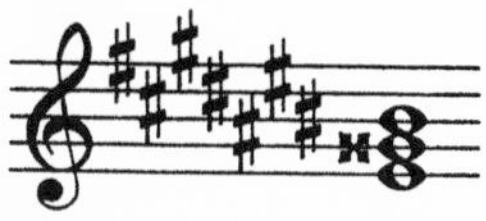

34 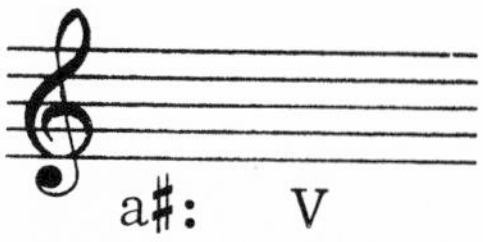    a#:   V

# Set 4  The major scale

Write the major scale *down* from the tonic D.
Mark the DST locations first.

34

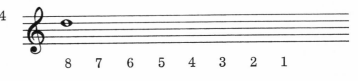

8    7    6    5    4    3    2    1

Write the descending A♭ major scale. *(Write the note numbers and mark the DST locations first, if you wish.)*

35

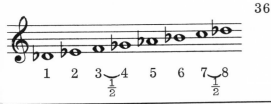

Occasionally it is necessary to work from a note other than the tonic. Using F as note 3 of a major scale, complete the scale in both directions. Mark the DST locations first:

36

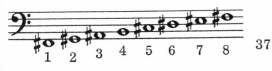

1   2   3   4   5   6   7   8

Using C♯ as note 5, complete the major scale in both directions:

37

1   2   3   4   5   6   7   8

is not

C♯ .......... (is *or* is not) the tonic of this scale.

38

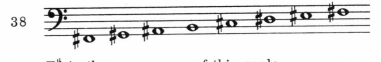

tonic

F♯ is the .......... of this scale.

Naming the notes of a scale or chord is called *spelling*. For example, the D major scale is spelled: D  E  F♯  G  A  B  C♯  D.
Spell the F major scale:

39

F G A B♭ C D E F

F __ __ __ __ __ __ F

20   Write d: V with key signature:

yes

21   Does VII contain note 7?  ___

22   Write  g: VII with key signature:

Write the indicated triads, with key signature:

23   f#:   III

24   bb:   V

25   g#:   VII

I, II, IV and VI

26   The triads *not* containing note 7 are  . . . . . . . . .

Facility in spelling major scales will prove valuable in later work. Spell *aloud* each of the following major scales, checking your answer after each scale. Repeat frames 40–56 until speed and assurance are felt. If spelling aloud is difficult for you, practice spelling the scales by writing them on a separate sheet of paper. When you can do this easily, go back to spelling aloud. You may find it helpful to think of the scale notes on a familiar instrument as you spell.

| | | | | | | | | | | |
|---|---|---|---|---|---|---|---|---|---|---|
| E  F♯  G♯  A  B  C♯  D♯  E | | | | E |
| B♭  C  D  E♭  F  G  A  B♭ | 41 | | B♭ |
| G♭  A♭  B♭  C♭  D♭  E♭  F  G♭ | 42 | | G♭ |
| A  B  C♯  D  E  F♯  G♯  A | 43 | | A |
| C♯  D♯  E♯  F♯  G♯  A♯  B♯  C♯ | 44 | | C♯ |
| E♭  F  G  A♭  B♭  C  D  E♭ | 45 | | E♭ |
| D♭  E♭  F  G♭  A♭  B♭  C  D♭ | 46 | | D♭ |
| G  A  B  C  D  E  F♯  G | 47 | | G |
| B  C♯  D♯  E  F♯  G♯  A♯  B | 48 | | B |
| F♭  G♭  A♭  B♭♭  C♭  D♭  E♭  F♭ | 49 | | F♭ |
| A♭  B♭  C  D♭  E♭  F  G  A♭ | 50 | | A♭ |
| D  E  F♯  G  A  B  C♯  D | 51 | | D |
| C  D  E  F  G  A  B  C | 52 | | C |
| F♯  G♯  A♯  B  C♯  D♯  E♯  F♯ | 53 | | F♯ |
| C♭  D♭  E♭  F♭  G♭  A♭  B♭  C♭ | 54 | | C♭ |
| F  G  A  B♭  C  D  E  F | 55 | | F |
| G♯  A♯  B♯  C♯  D♯  E♯  F𝄪  G♯ | 56 | | G♯ |

40

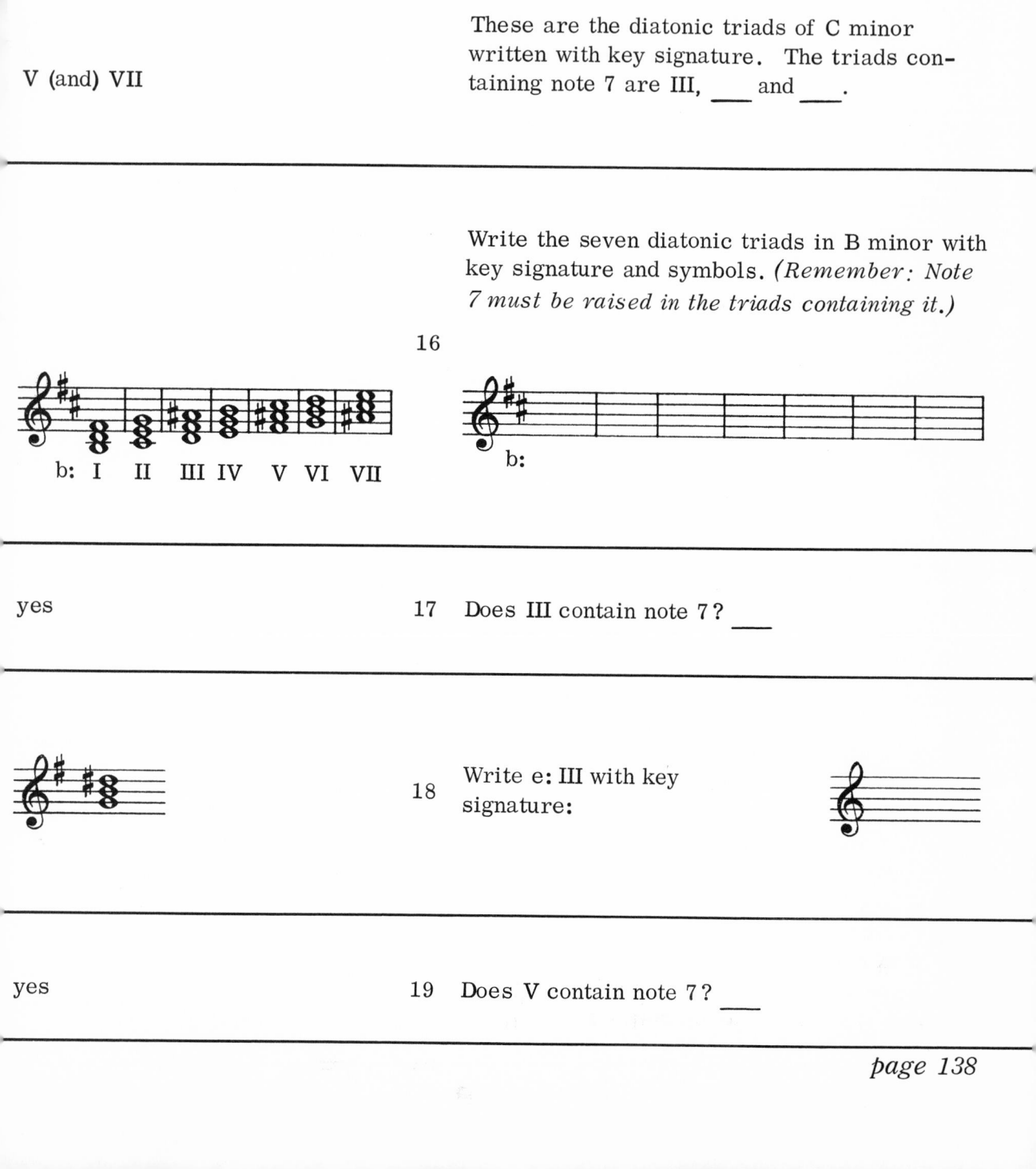

V (and) VII

15  c:  I   II   III   IV   V   VI   VII

These are the diatonic triads of C minor written with key signature. The triads containing note 7 are III, ___ and ___.

Write the seven diatonic triads in B minor with key signature and symbols. *(Remember: Note 7 must be raised in the triads containing it.)*

16

b: I   II   III IV   V   VI   VII

b:

yes

17  Does III contain note 7? ___

18  Write e: III with key signature:

yes

19  Does V contain note 7? ___

| | | |
|---|---|---|
| interval | 1 | The relationship between two pitches is called an *interval*. Between any two notes there is a pitch relationship or an _____ . |
| relationship<br>*(Was your answer distance? The next few frames show why* rela-*tionship is preferred.)* | 2 | An interval is the _____ between two pitches. |
| close together | 3 | Intervals vary in size. Two pitches that are far apart form a large interval. A small interval is formed by two pitches that are . . . . . . . . . . . |
| larger *(or greater)* | 4 | The greater the distance between two pitches, the _____ the interval. |
| (1) smaller<br><br>(2) larger | 5 | Interval y is slightly (1)_____ (larger *or* smaller) than interval x, and interval z is slightly (2)_____ than interval x.<br><br>x  y  z |
| (1) smaller *(either order)*<br>(2) larger | 6 | Interval y is smaller than interval x and sounds harsh compared to interval x. Interval z is larger than interval x and *also* sounds harsh compared to it. This shows that the harsher of two intervals is sometimes the (1) _____ interval and sometimes the (2) _____ interval. |

do not

8    Harmonic minor scales ......... (do *or* do not) correspond to the minor key signatures.

Write the signature of D minor followed by the D harmonic minor scale:

9

accidental

10    A sign not belonging to the key signature is a(n) _____ .

(1) 7
(2) raised

11    When a harmonic minor scale is written with key signature, note (1) ___ of the scale must be (2) _____ (raised *or* lowered) by an accidental.

Write the Ab harmonic minor scale, with key signature:

12

(1) diatonic
(2) harmonic minor

13    In the minor keys, (1) _____ triads are derived from the (2) ......... scale.

(1) 7
(2) raised


(3) 7
(4) raised

14    When the harmonic minor scale is written with key signature, note (1) ___ must be (2) _____ . Therefore, when diatonic triads in minor keys are written with key signature, note (3) ___ of the scale must be (4) _____ in those triads containing it.

**7**

As shown above, the sound of an interval is not simply a matter of size. For this and other reasons it is not quite right to say that an interval is the *distance* between two pitches. It is better to say that an interval is the

_____ _____ _____ _____

elationship between
wo pitches

---

x          y

**8**

Two pitches sounded together form a harmonic interval. Two pitches sounded consecutively form a melodic interval. Interval x is a
(1) _____ interval. Interval y is a
(2) _____ interval. (For the sake of consistency, all intervals in this part of the book are written as harmonic intervals.)

1) melodic
2) harmonic

---

**9**

Every interval has a *general name*. Ordinal numbers (2nd, 3rd, 4th, etc.) are used as general names. 5th is the _____ name of an interval.

eneral

---

2nd  3rd  4th  5th  6th  7th  x  y

**10**

The general name of an interval is found by counting *inclusively* the lines and spaces from one note to the other. Shown above are some intervals and their general names. The general name of interval x is (1) _____.
Interval y is a (2) _____.

(1) 3rd
(2) 4th

---

Give the general names of these intervals:

**11**

(1)      (2)      (3)      (4)

(1) 6th
(2) 2nd
(3) 5th
(4) 9th

**(1) major**

**(2) harmonic minor**

1

Authorities differ on the question of which minor scales are diatonic scales, and which triads are diatonic triads in the minor keys. But one thing seems certain: In the minor keys the vast majority of triads correspond to the *harmonic* minor scale. It is therefore convenient to define diatonic triads in minor as triads derived from the harmonic minor scale. In the major keys, diatonic triads are derived from the (1) ......... scale. In the minor keys, diatonic triads are derived from the (2) ......... scale.

---

diatonic

2

Triads derived from the C harmonic minor scale are the _____ triads in C minor.

---

E minor

3

Minor keys are symbolized by small letters. e: I means I in the key of ___ _____.

---

Write the proper symbol beneath each of the following chords. In each case assume the minor key corresponding to the given signature.

4

c: II

---

d: IV

5

---

f♯: V

6

---

f: VII

7

**12** Instead of the number "1st" the word *prime* is used as a general name. Instead of the number "8th" the word *octave* is used. Give the general names of these intervals:

1) prime
2) octave
3) 7th
4) prime

**13** In finding the general name of an interval, sharps and flats may be ignored. The general name of intervals s, t and w, is 3rd. Intervals x, y and z all have the general name

_____.

th

**14** The general name of an interval gives only a rough idea (a "general" idea) of its size. Two intervals that are not exactly the same_____ may have the same general name.

ize

**15** An interval is the (1) _____ _____ _____ _____. The general name of an interval gives a rough idea of its (2)_____ .

1) relationship between two pitches
2) size

**16** Give the general names of these intervals:

(1) 2nd
(2) octave
(3) 4th
(4) prime

**17** The number of lines and spaces from one note to another, inclusive of both, determines the _____ name of an interval.

general

Give the structural types of the other five diatonic triads in C:

III  IV  V  VI  VII
min maj maj min dim

40

|     | I   | II  | III | IV  | V   | VI  | VII |
|-----|-----|-----|-----|-----|-----|-----|-----|
|     | maj | min | ___ | ___ | ___ | ___ | ___ |

scale

41  Diatonic triads are derived from a _____ .

major

42  All major scales have the same structure. Therefore, a diatonic triad from one major scale (or key) has the same structure as the corresponding diatonic triad from another scale (or key).  C: I is a major triad.  G: I is a major triad.  D: I is a major triad, etc.  In *any* major key, I is a(n) _____ triad.

(1) minor
(2) minor

43  Since C: II is a(n) (1) _____ triad, II is a(n) (2) _____ triad in any major key.

Complete the structural description of diatonic triads in major keys:

III  min
IV  maj
V  maj
VI  min
VII  dim

44

| I   | maj |
|-----|-----|
| II  | min |
| III | ___ |
| IV  | ___ |
| V   | ___ |
| VI  | ___ |
| VII | ___ |

(*Hint: Remember the form of the previous item: "Since C: II is a minor triad......"*)

(1) IV (and) V
(2) II, III (and) VI
(3) VII

45  In any major key, I, (1) ___ and ___, are major triads; (2) ___, ___ and ___, are minor triads; and (3) ___ is a diminished triad.

| | | |
|---|---|---|
| 1) prime<br>2) octave | 18 | Most general names are ordinal numbers, but the word (1) _____ is used instead of "1st," and the word (2) _____ is used instead of "8th." |
| rime | 19 | Both intervals have the general name _____. |
| hromatic | 20 | This interval is one kind of prime. It is called a _____ semitone. |
| 2nd | 21 | Both intervals have the general name _____. |
| diatonic | 22 | This interval is one kind of 2nd. It is called a _____ semitone. |
| whole tone | 23 | This interval is another kind of 2nd. It is called a_____ _____. |
| (1) 2nd<br>(2) prime<br>(3) 2nd | 24 | A DST is one kind of (1)_____.(gen. name)<br>A CST is one kind of (2)_____.(gen. name)<br>A whole tone is one kind of (3)_____.(gen. name) |

Write the indicated triads *without key signatures:*

31 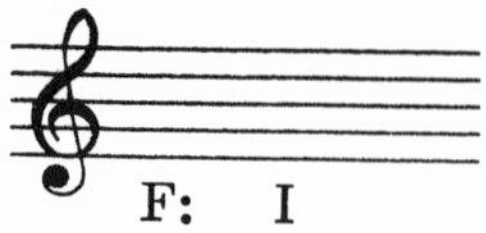    F:   I

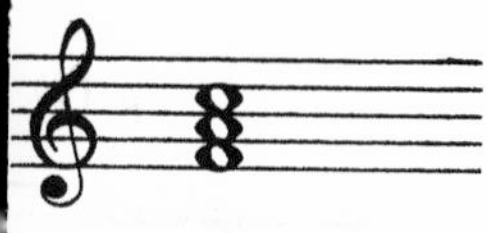

32 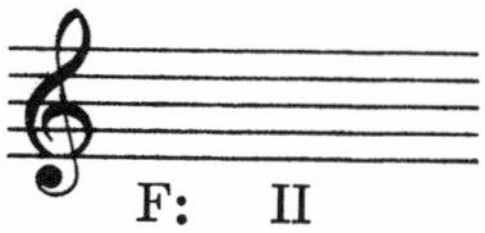    F:   II

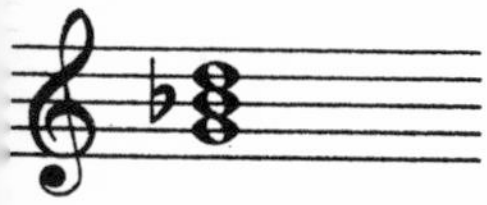

33 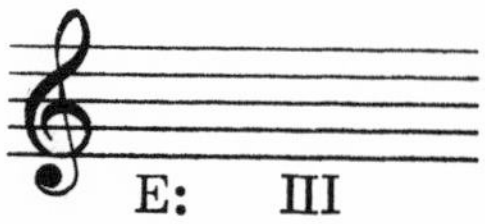    E:   III

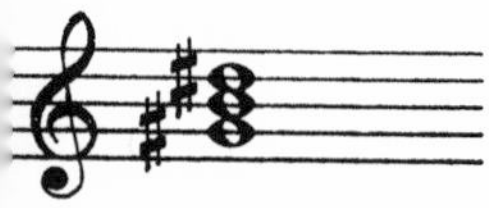

34 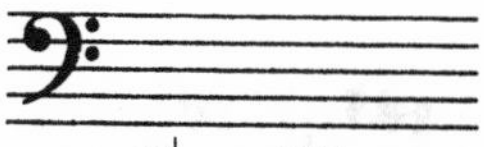    G♭:  VI

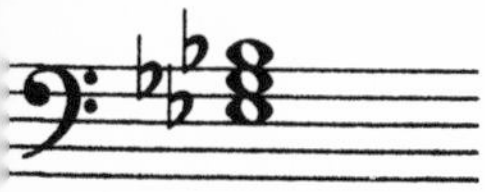

35    F♯:  VI

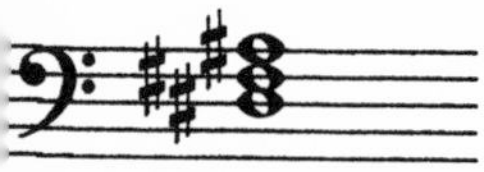

F  A♭  C        36    Spell D♭: III: ___ ___ ___

G♯  B  D♯       37    Spell B: VI: ___ ___ ___

maj             38 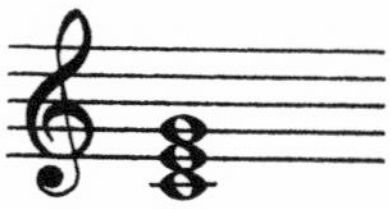    C: I is a _____ triad.
                      *(What structural type?)*

min             39 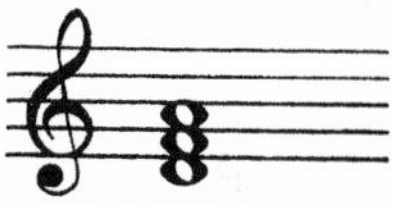    The structural type of C: II is
                      _____.

25  Raising (or lowering) both notes of an interval *equally* does not change the size of the interval. If both notes of interval x are raised one CST, we have interval y. The size of the interval ........... (is *or* is not) changed.

s not

ιe same
*or* equal in
*or* of equal)

26

Lowering both notes of interval x one CST makes interval y. Intervals x and y are .......... size.

Fill in the upper note of interval y, making interval y the same size as interval x.
*(Hint: What must be done to the lower note of x to change it to the lower note of y?)*

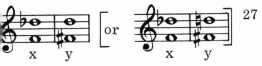 27

*(Each note of x is raised one CST to make y.)*

28  Fill in the lower note of interval y, making interval y the same size as interval x:

29  Raising or lowering only *one* note of an interval *does* change the size of the interval. An interval may be expanded by raising the _____ (upper *or* lower) note.

upper

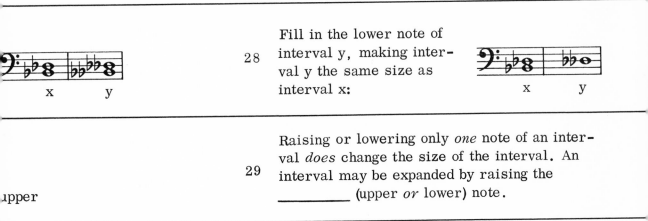

# Set 21 Diatonic triads in major

25

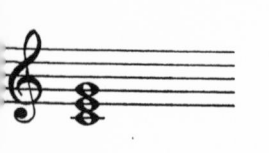

Write C: I:

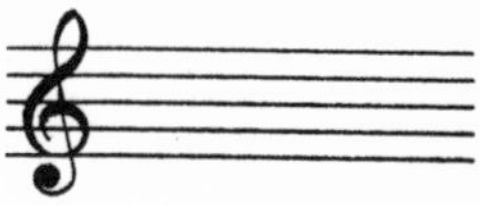

*(In all answers of this kind the entire chord may be written an octave higher or lower than shown.)*

Write the indicated triads, using the appropriate key signature in each case:

26

B♭: II

27

D: III

28

E♭: VII

29

A♭: V

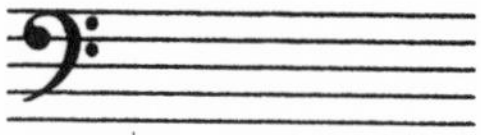

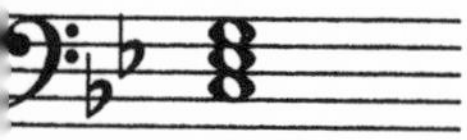

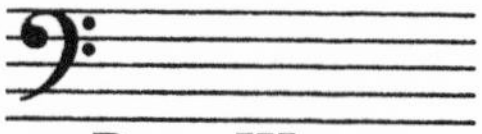

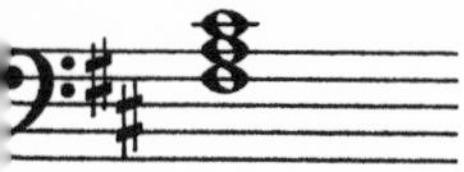

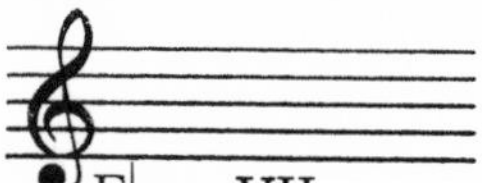

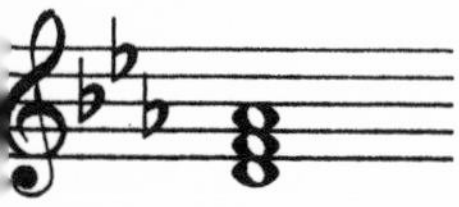

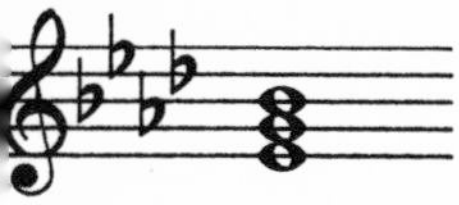

30

A: V

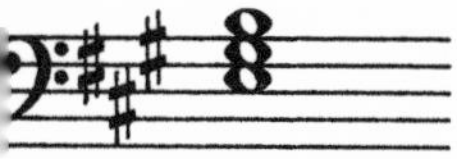

| | | |
|---|---|---|
| owering | 30 | An interval may be expanded by _____ (raising *or* lowering) the lower note. |

| | | |
|---|---|---|
| (1) expands<br><br>(2) contracts | 31 | Raising the upper note one CST (1) _____ (expands *or* contracts) the interval one CST. Raising the lower note one CST (2) _____ the interval one CST. |

| | | |
|---|---|---|
| (1) expand<br>(2) one CST | 32 | Placing a sharp before F would (1) _____ the interval (2) ......... (how much?) |

| | | |
|---|---|---|
| D | 33 | Placing a flat before ___ would expand the interval one CST. |

| | | |
|---|---|---|
|  | 34 | Expand this interval one CST by changing the sign of the upper note. (The "sign" of the upper note as it stands is an understood ♮.) |

| | | |
|---|---|---|
|  | 35 | Expand this interval one CST by changing the sign of the lower note: |

| | | |
|---|---|---|
| larger | 36 | Interval x is one CST _____ (larger *or* smaller) than interval y. |

Write the proper symbol under each of the following chords.  In each case assume the major key corresponding to the given signature.

17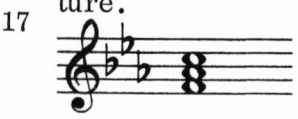

Eb: II

18

B: III

19

A: V

20

Db: I

21

C#: IV

diatonic

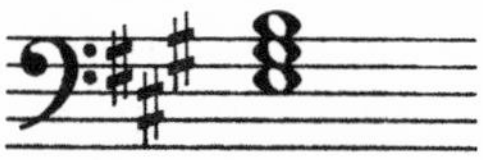

22 Triads derived from a scale are _____ triads.

degrees

23 Notes of a scale serving as chord roots are called _____.

(1) diatonic triad
(2) 4th degree
(3) C major

24 The symbol C: IV stands for a (1) _____ _____built on the (2) .......... in the key of (3) ___ _____.

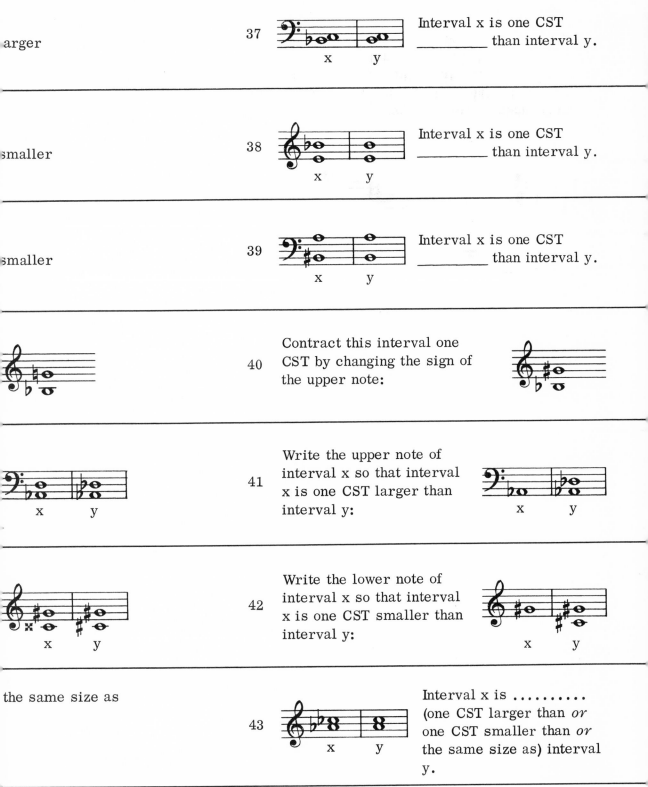

arger

**37**    Interval x is one CST
_____ than interval y.

smaller

**38**    Interval x is one CST
_____ than interval y.

smaller

**39**    Interval x is one CST
_____ than interval y.

**40**    Contract this interval one
CST by changing the sign of
the upper note:

**41**    Write the upper note of
interval x so that interval
x is one CST larger than
interval y:

**42**    Write the lower note of
interval x so that interval
x is one CST smaller than
interval y:

the same size as

**43**    Interval x is .........
(one CST larger than *or*
one CST smaller than *or*
the same size as) interval
y.

# Set 21 Diatonic triads in major

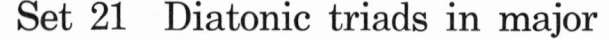

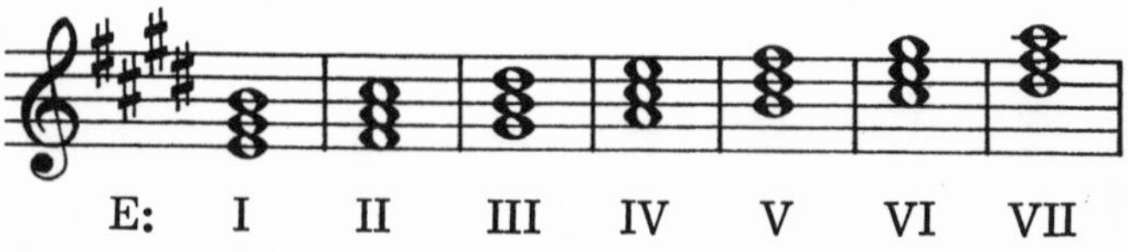
E: I II III IV V VI VII

12 Roman numerals corresponding to degrees are used as symbols for diatonic triads. Shown above are the seven diatonic triads in E major and their symbols. The (1) ________ triad whose root is the (2) ________ ________ has the symbol VI.

(1) diatonic
(2) 6th degree

---

13 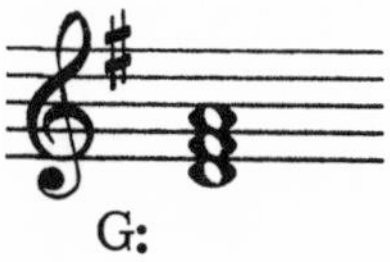
G:

The root of this chord, D, is the ________ ________ in the key of G. Write the chord symbol under the chord.

5th degree

V

---

14 Write the chord symbol:

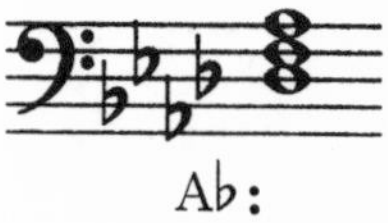
A♭:

IV

---

15 Roman numerals symbolize ________ triads.

diatonic

---

x 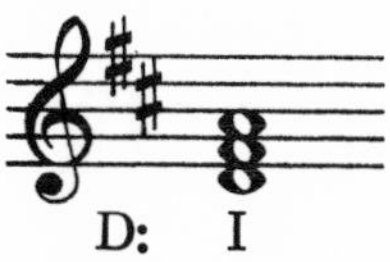
D: I

y 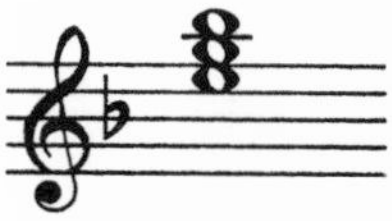

16 When used as a key symbol, C means C major, C# means C# major, etc. Major keys are symbolized by capital letters. Thus, the complete symbol for chord x is D: I. Chord y is in the key of F major. Write the complete chord symbol under chord y.

F: VII

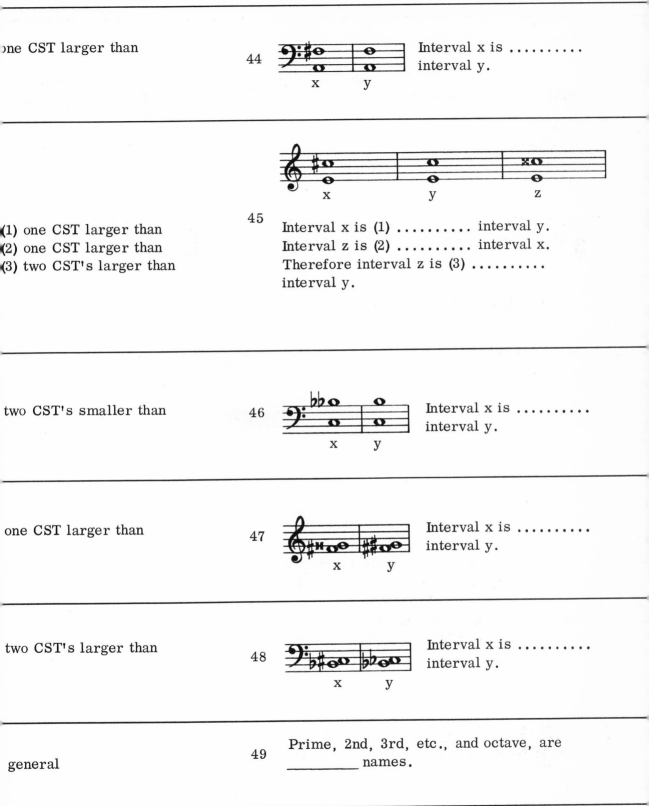

one CST larger than

44    Interval x is .......... interval y.

(1) one CST larger than
(2) one CST larger than
(3) two CST's larger than

45    Interval x is (1) .......... interval y.
Interval z is (2) .......... interval x.
Therefore interval z is (3) ..........
interval y.

two CST's smaller than

46    Interval x is .......... interval y.

one CST larger than

47    Interval x is .......... interval y.

two CST's larger than

48    Interval x is .......... interval y.

general

49    Prime, 2nd, 3rd, etc., and octave, are _____ names.

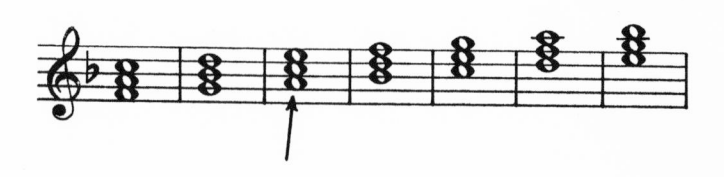

3rd degree

8

Notes of a scale serving as roots are called *degrees*. The expression *2nd degree* means note 2 of a scale serving as the root of a chord. The indicated note is the _____ _____ in the key of F major.

---

roots

9

Notes of a scale serving as _____ are called degrees.

---

Draw an arrow pointing to the 6th degree:

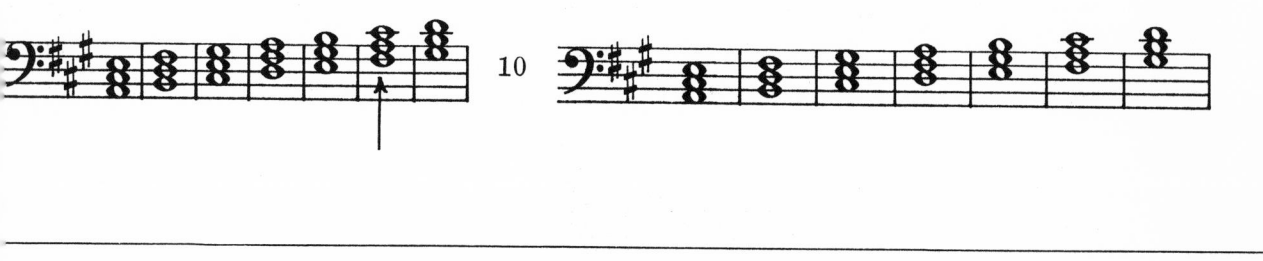

10

---

(1) diatonic
(2) A major

11

Above are the seven (1) _____ triads in the key of (2) _____.

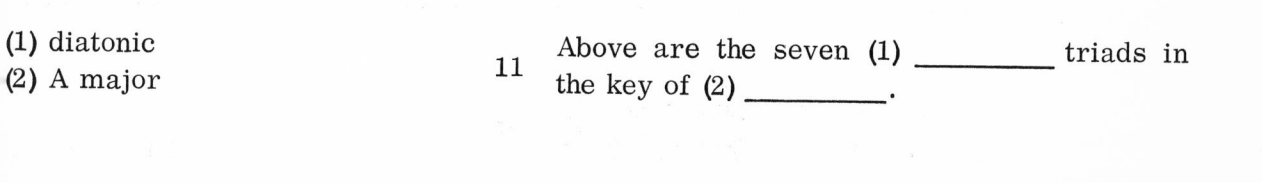

**1**

All intervals have double names. The double names consist of a *specific* name followed by a *general* name. In the double name *major 3rd*, the word *major* is the (1) _____ name, and *3rd* is the (2) _____ name.

(1) specific
(2) general

**2**

Another example of a double name is *minor 6th*. *Major* and *minor* are (1) _____ names. *3rd* and *6th* are (2) _____ names. *Major 3rd* and *minor 6th* are (3) _____ names.

(1) specific
(2) general
(3) double

**3**

Every interval has a (1) _____ name, consisting of a (2) _____ name followed by a (3) _____ name.

(1) double
(2) specific
(3) general

**4**

Double names refer to exact interval sizes. The name *7th*, by itself, gives only a (1) _____ idea of interval size, but *major 7th* refers to an (2) _____ interval size.

(1) rough (*or* general)
(2) exact

**5**

The first step in finding the specific name of an interval is to construct a major scale on the lower note of the interval, as shown below for interval x. Complete this step for interval y.

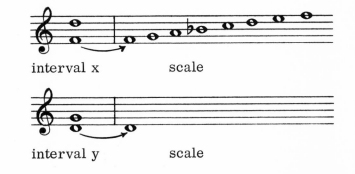

interval x          scale

interval y          scale

major scales

**4** Since major key signatures correspond to
_____ _____, the triads derived from a
major scale may be written with a key signature and no accidentals. The triads derived
from the D major scale are shown in this way
above. Write the key signature for B♭ major
and the triads derived from the B♭ major
scale:

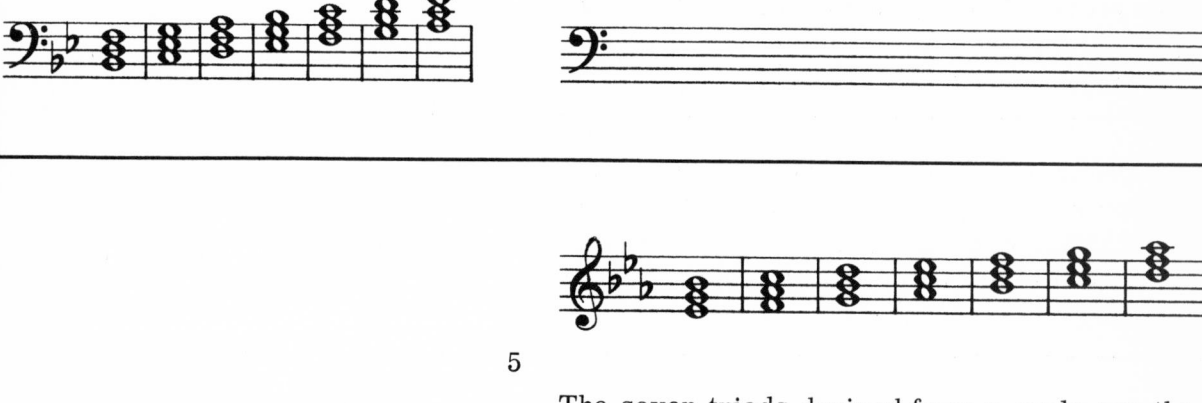

**5**

The seven triads derived from a scale are the
*diatonic triads* in the corresponding key.
Shown above are the seven (1) _____
_____ in the key of (2)___ _____.

(1) diatonic triads
(2) E♭ major

scale

**6** Diatonic triads are derived from a _____.

diatonic

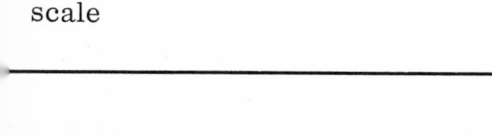

**7**

These are two of the seven _____ triads in
the key of F♯ major. Write the other five.

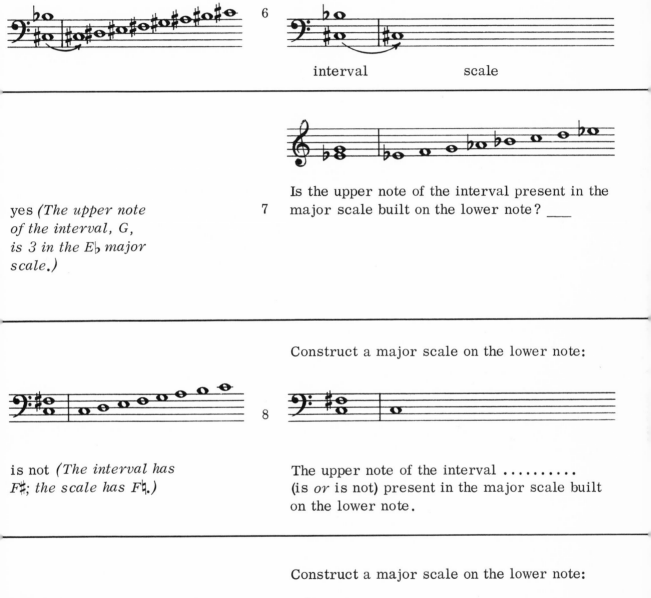

Construct a major scale on the lower note
of the following interval:

6

interval          scale

yes *(The upper note
of the interval, G,
is 3 in the E♭ major
scale.)*

7   Is the upper note of the interval present in the
major scale built on the lower note? ___

Construct a major scale on the lower note:

8

is not *(The interval has
F♯; the scale has F♮.)*

The upper note of the interval .........
(is *or* is not) present in the major scale built
on the lower note.

Construct a major scale on the lower note:

9

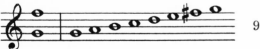

no

Does the upper note of the interval match a
note in the scale? ___

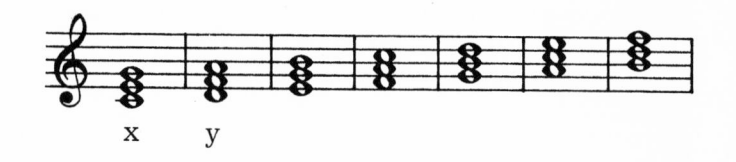

x    y

1

root

These are the seven triads derived from the C major scale. The tonic is the root of triad x. Note 2 is the root of triad y. Each note of the scale is used, in turn, as the _____ of a triad.

---

2

A♭
major scale

These triads are derived from the ___ _____ _____.

---

Shown below is one of the triads derived from the G major scale. Write the other triads derived from the G major scale. Do not use a key signature.

3

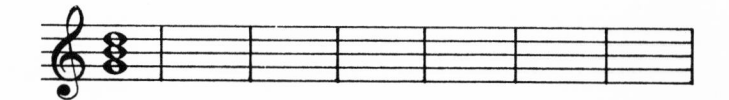

Construct a major scale on the lower note:

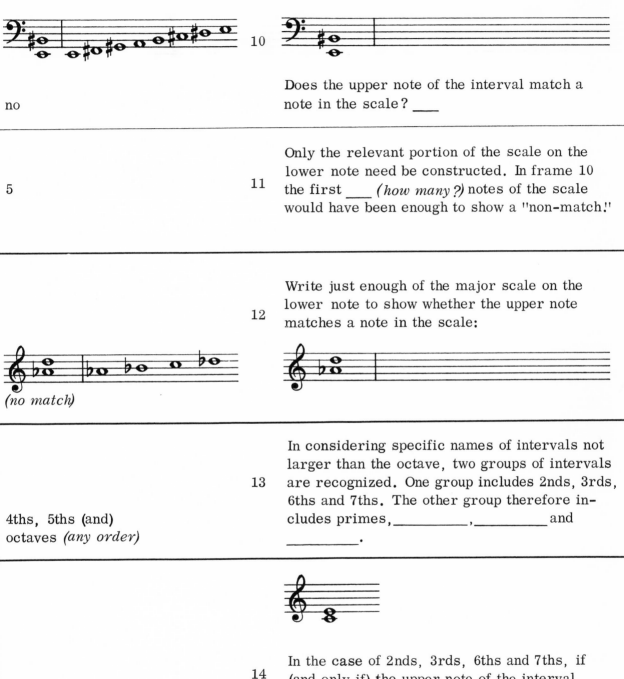

10

Does the upper note of the interval match a note in the scale? ___

no

11

Only the relevant portion of the scale on the lower note need be constructed. In frame 10 the first ___ *(how many?)* notes of the scale would have been enough to show a "non-match!"

5

12

Write just enough of the major scale on the lower note to show whether the upper note matches a note in the scale:

*(no match)*

13

In considering specific names of intervals not larger than the octave, two groups of intervals are recognized. One group includes 2nds, 3rds, 6ths and 7ths. The other group therefore includes primes,_____,_____and _____.

4ths, 5ths (and)
octaves *(any order)*

14

In the case of 2nds, 3rds, 6ths and 7ths, if (and only if) the upper note of the interval matches a note in the major scale built on the lower note, the specific name is *major*. The above interval has the specific name _____.

major

# Set 20 The structure of triads (2)

Write the indicated triads:

30 C♯ min triad:

31 B♭ dim triad:

F A C♯  32 Spell an F aug triad: F ___ ___

A♭ C E♭  33 Spell an A♭ maj triad: A♭ ___ ___

Write the four different types of triad, using E as the *root* in each case:

34

maj min aug dim

Write the four different types of triad, using E♯ as the *third* in each case:

35

maj min aug dim

Write the four different types of triad, using F as the *fifth* in each case:

36

maj min aug dim

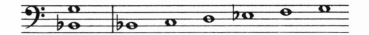

**(1) upper**

**(2) lower**
**(3) major**

15   The (1) _____ note of the interval matches
a note in the major scale built on the
(2) _____ note. Therefore, the specific
name is (3) _____ .

---

16

From this point on you should try to *spell*
(silently or aloud) the major scales needed for
interval work. Spell the scales on paper or
write out the notes (on a separate sheet of
music paper) only when you feel it necessary.

**(1) does (The major
scale on the lower
note goes G A B C D E.)**

**(2) is**

The upper note (1) .........
(does *or* does not) match a note
in the major scale built on the
lower note. Therefore the
specific name (2) .........
(is *or* is not) major.

---

**(1) does not (The major
scale on the lower note
goes D♭ E♭ F G♭ A♭ B♭.)**
**(2) is not**

17

The upper note (1) .........
match a note in the major
scale built on the lower note.
The specific name (2) .........
major.

---

**is**

18

The specific name .........
major.

---

**is not**

19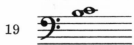

The specific name .........
major.

---

# Set 20 The structure of triads (2)

Label each triad maj, min, dim or aug:

dim — 22 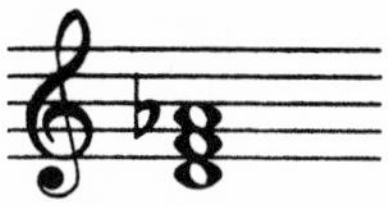 ________

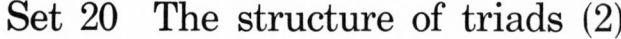

min — 23 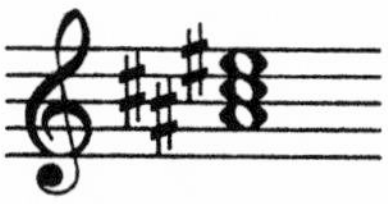 ________

aug — 24 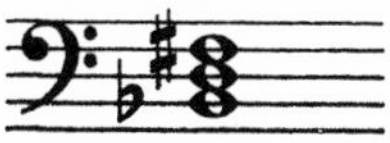 ________

dim — 25 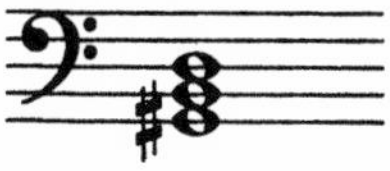 ________

Label each triad maj, min, dim or aug:

min — 26 E♭ G♭ B♭ ________

maj — 27 B D♯ F♯ ________

aug — 28 G B D♯ ________

maj — 29 B♭♭ D♭ F♭ ________

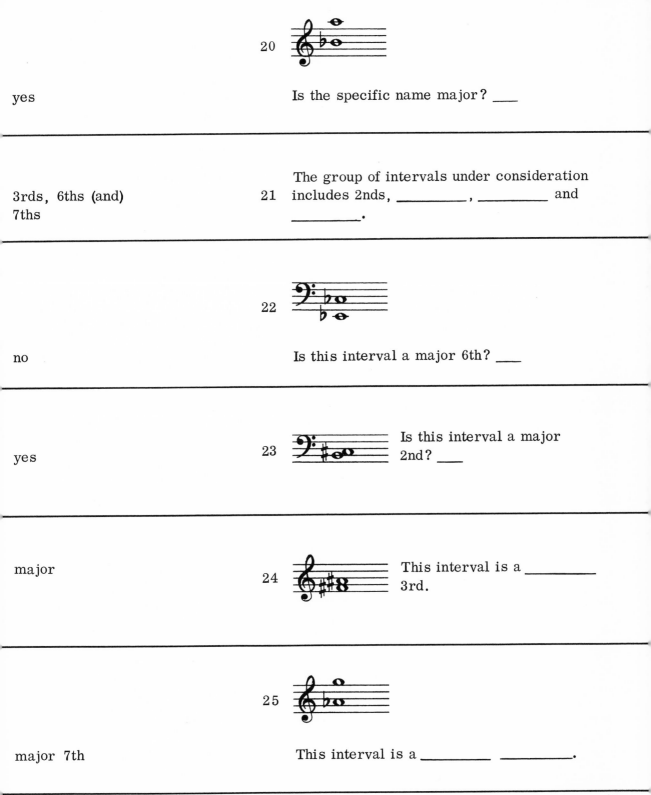

yes

20

Is the specific name major? ___

3rds, 6ths (and)
7ths

21 The group of intervals under consideration includes 2nds, _____, _____ and _____.

22

no

Is this interval a major 6th? ___

yes

23

Is this interval a major 2nd? ___

major

24

This interval is a _____ 3rd.

25

major 7th

This interval is a _____ _____.

(1) 3rds
(2) triad

18   A chord of three notes built in (1) _____
is a (2) _____ .

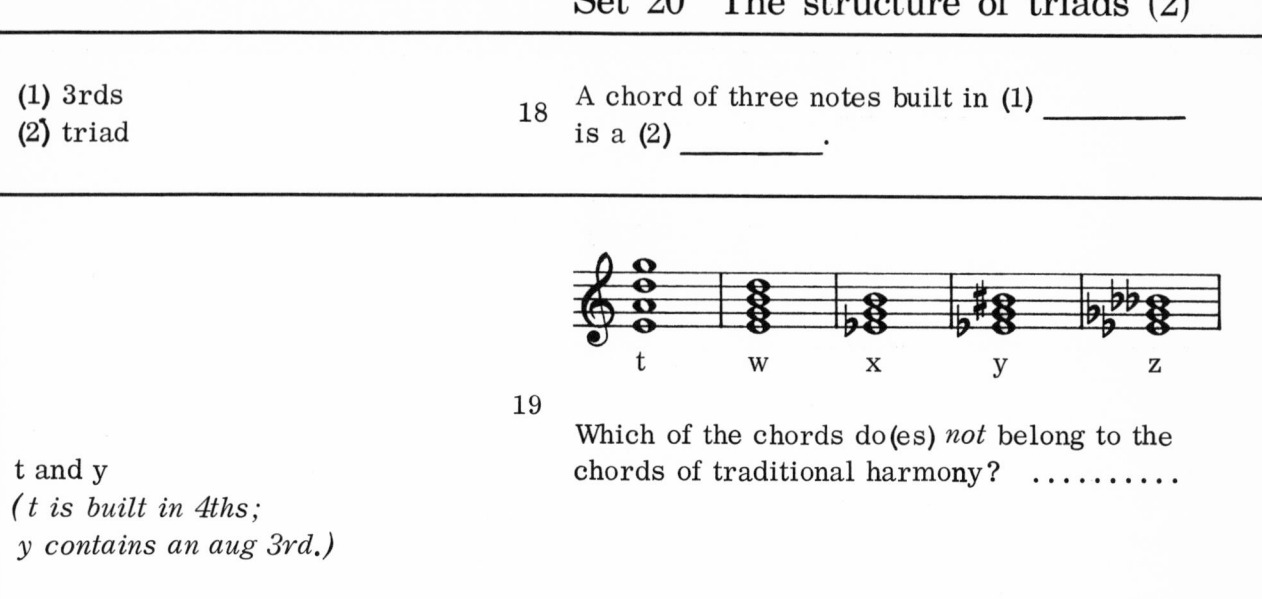

19

Which of the chords do(es) *not* belong to the chords of traditional harmony?   ..........

t and y
*( t is built in 4ths;
y contains an aug 3rd.)*

Show the structure of major and minor triads by filling in the blanks:

min            maj
     perf           perf
maj            min

20

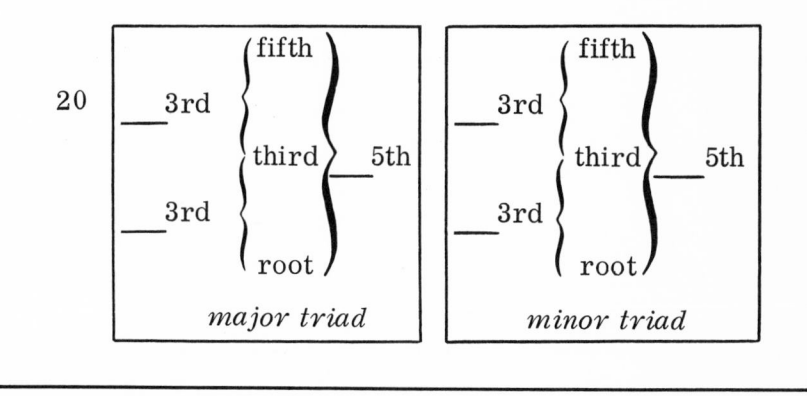

*major triad*      *minor triad*

Fill in the blanks:

min            maj
     dim            aug
min            maj

21

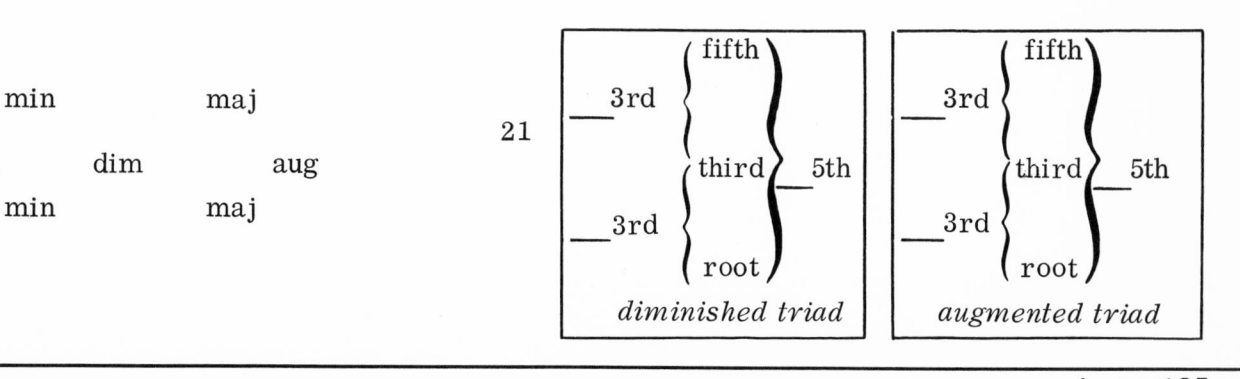

*diminished triad*      *augmented triad*

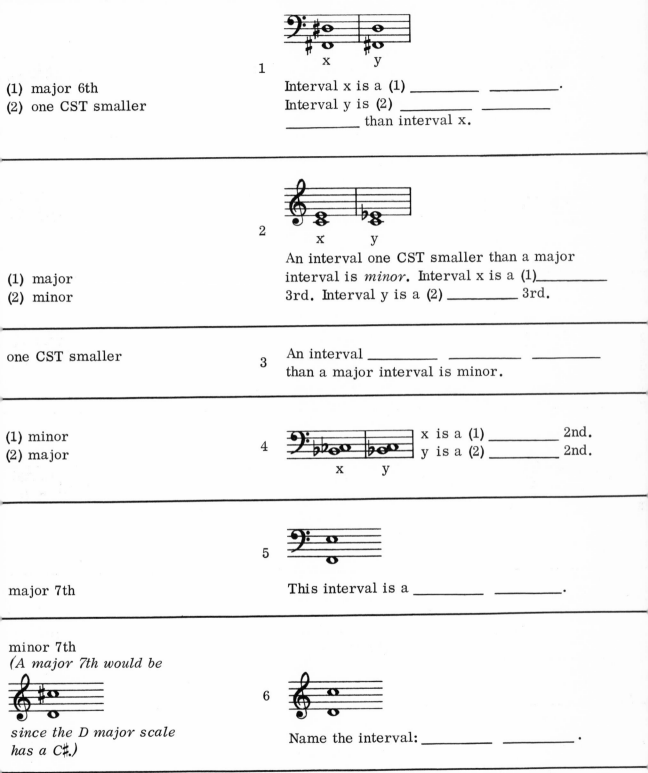

**1**

(1) major 6th
(2) one CST smaller

Interval x is a (1) _____ _____ .
Interval y is (2) _____ _____
_____ than interval x.

**2**

(1) major
(2) minor

An interval one CST smaller than a major
interval is *minor*. Interval x is a (1)_____
3rd. Interval y is a (2) _____ 3rd.

one CST smaller

**3**

An interval _____ _____ _____
than a major interval is minor.

(1) minor
(2) major

**4**

x is a (1) _____ 2nd.
y is a (2) _____ 2nd.

**5**

major 7th

This interval is a _____ _____ .

minor 7th
*(A major 7th would be*

*since the D major scale
has a C♯.)*

**6**

Name the interval: _____ _____ .

# Set 20 The structure of triads (2)

root
(and) fifth

12 Diminished and augmented triads take their names from the interval between ________ and ________.

(1) dim

(2) aug

13 


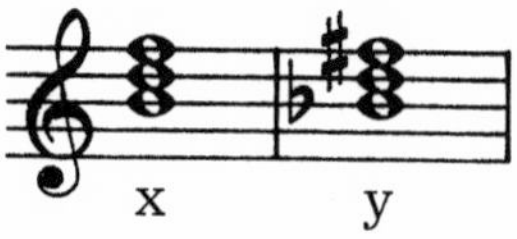

Chord x is a(n) (1)________ triad.
Chord y is a(n) (2)________ triad.

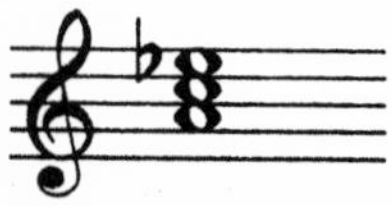

Write the following triads:

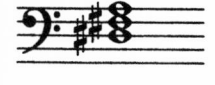

14 dim triad on the root A:

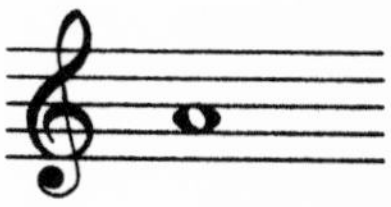

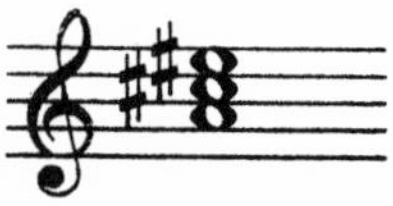

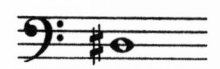

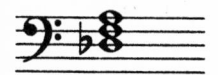

15 A aug triad:

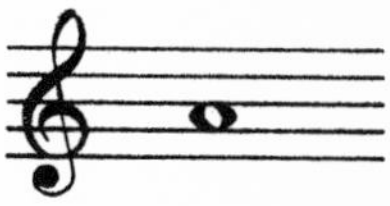

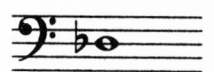

16 D♯ dim triad:

17 D♭ aug triad:

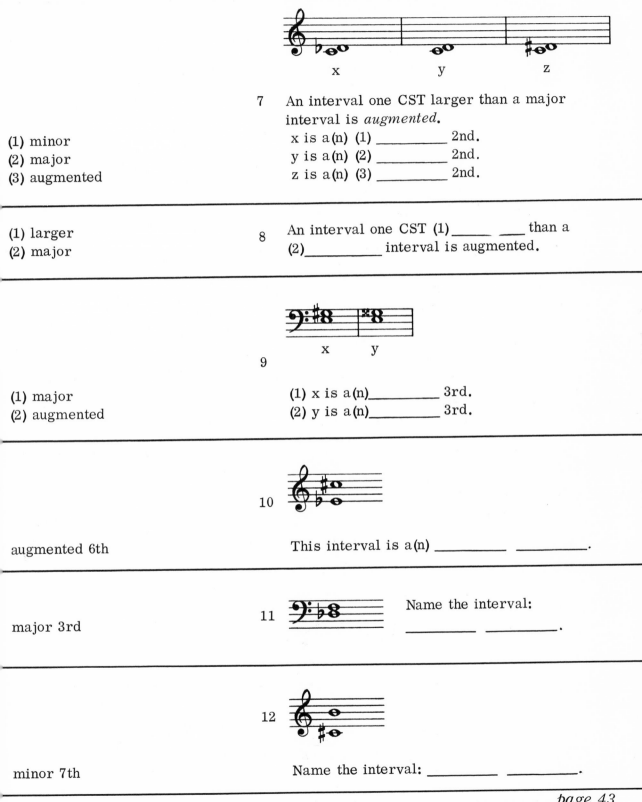

**7** An interval one CST larger than a major interval is *augmented*.

x is a(n) (1) _____ 2nd.
y is a(n) (2) _____ 2nd.
z is a(n) (3) _____ 2nd.

(1) minor
(2) major
(3) augmented

**8** An interval one CST (1) _____ than a (2) _____ interval is augmented.

(1) larger
(2) major

**9**

(1) x is a(n) _____ 3rd.
(2) y is a(n) _____ 3rd.

(1) major
(2) augmented

**10** This interval is a(n) _____ _____.

augmented 6th

**11** Name the interval: _____ _____.

major 3rd

**12** Name the interval: _____ _____.

minor 7th

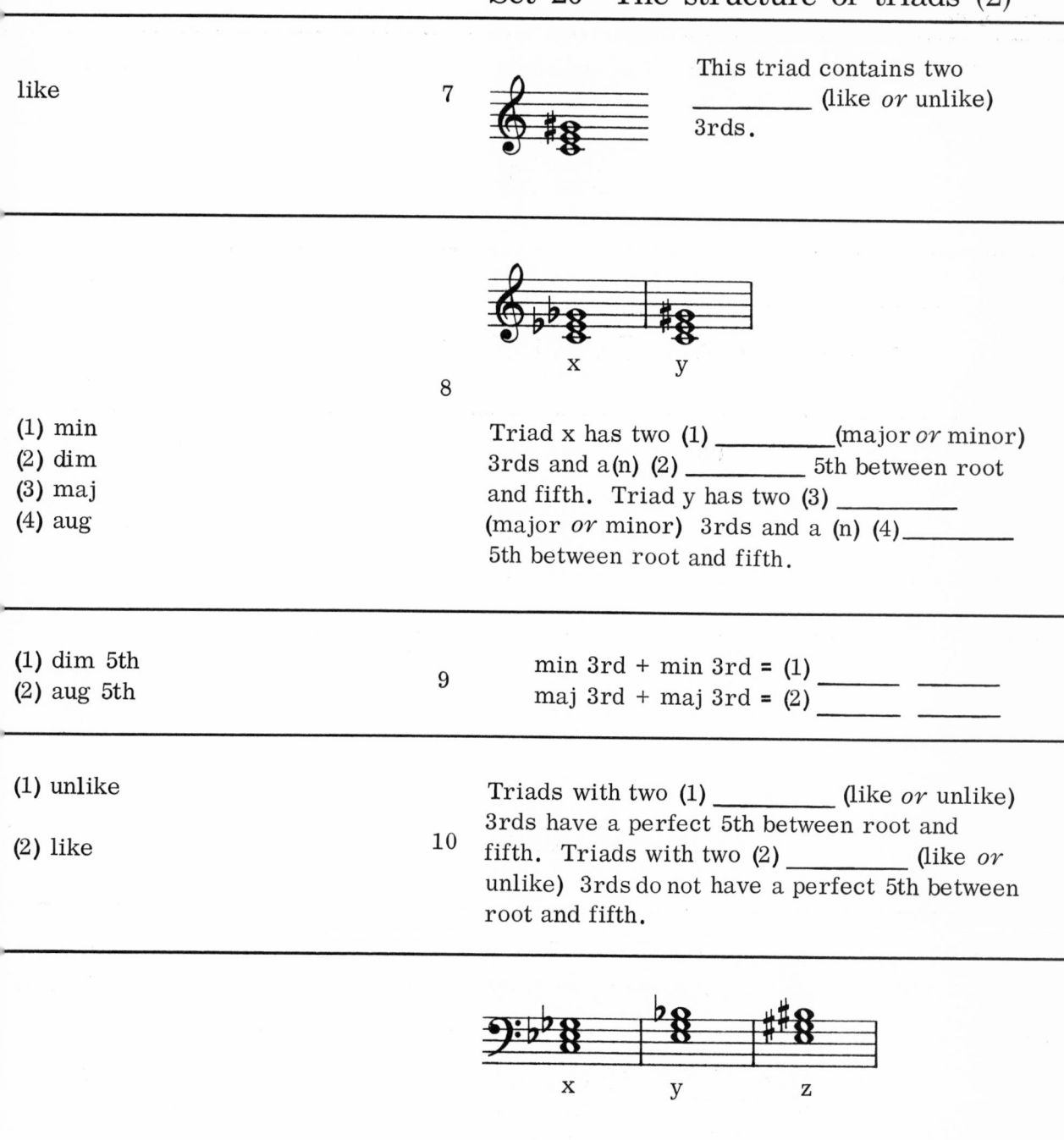

like

7   This triad contains two
    _____ (like *or* unlike)
    3rds.

8

(1) min    Triad x has two (1) _____ (major *or* minor)
(2) dim    3rds and a(n) (2) _____ 5th between root
(3) maj    and fifth. Triad y has two (3) _____
(4) aug    (major *or* minor) 3rds and a (n) (4) _____
           5th between root and fifth.

(1) dim 5th    9    min 3rd + min 3rd = (1) _____ _____
(2) aug 5th         maj 3rd + maj 3rd = (2) _____ _____

(1) unlike    Triads with two (1) _____ (like *or* unlike)
              3rds have a perfect 5th between root and
              fifth. Triads with two (2) _____ (like *or*
(2) like   10 unlike) 3rds do not have a perfect 5th between
              root and fifth.

11   Triads with two *like* 3rds take their names
     from the interval between root and fifth. Since
     triad x has a diminished 5th between root and
     fifth, it is a *diminished triad*. Triad y is a(n)
(1) dim   (1) _____ triad. Triad z is a(n)
(2) aug   (2) _____ triad.

w    x    y    z

**13**   An interval one CST smaller than a minor interval is *diminished*.

(1) diminished

(2) minor

(3) major

(4) augmented

w is a(n) (1) _____ 6th.

x is a(n) (2) _____ 6th.

y is a(n) (3) _____ 6th.

z is a(n) (4) _____ 6th.

---

(1) smaller

(2) minor

**14**   An interval one CST (1) _____ than a (2) _____ interval is diminished.

---

(1) diminished

(2) minor

**15**

x    y

x is a(n) (1) _____ 3rd.

y is a(n) (2) _____ 3rd.

---

(1) min

(2) aug

(3) dim

(In the interest of speed, the usual period following an abbreviation may be omitted.)

**16**   The first three letters of each of these terms — major, minor, augmented and diminished — will serve as an abbreviation. The abbreviation for major is maj. The abbreviation for minor is (1) _____. Augmented is abbreviated (2) _____, and diminished is abbreviated (3) _____.

---

dim   min   maj   aug

**17**   Arrange maj, min, aug and dim, in order, from smallest to largest:

_____ _____ _____ _____

---

dim 7th

**18**   Name the following intervals:

_____ _____

unlike

1  Since a major triad contains a major 3rd and a minor 3rd we may say that it has two *unlike* 3rds. A minor triad also contains a major 3rd and minor 3rd (though not in the same relative position). A minor triad has two _____ thirds.

unlike

2  Both major triads and minor triads are composed of two_____ 3rds.

Construct the indicated triads:

3  C major triad     C minor triad

(1) perfect
(2) perfect

Examination of these two triads shows that a major triad has a(n) (1) _____ 5th between root and fifth. A minor triad has a(n) (2)_____ 5th between root and fifth.

unlike

4  Triads with two _____3rds have a perfect 5th between root and fifth

perf 5th

5     maj 3rd + min 3rd = _____  _____

like

6  This triad contains two _____ (like *or* unlike) 3rds.

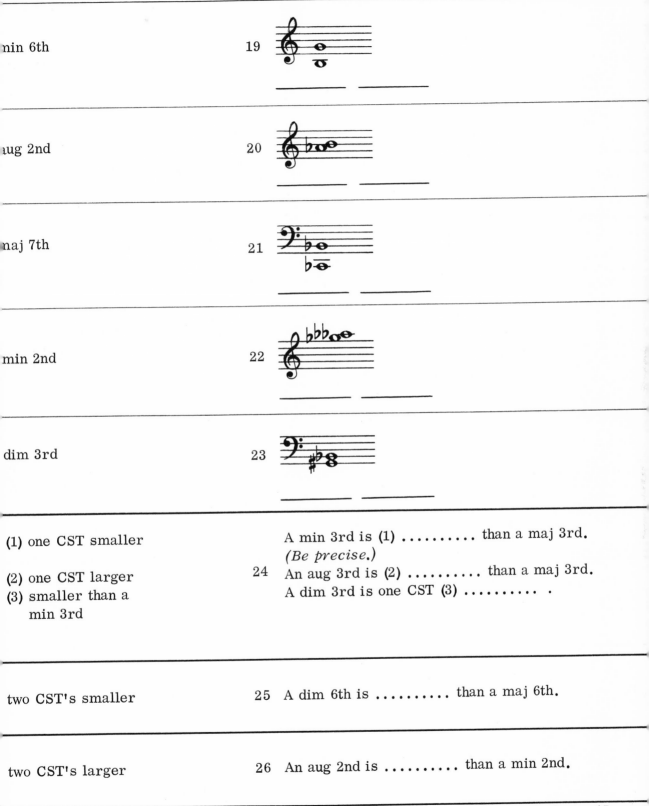

min 6th | 19

aug 2nd | 20

maj 7th | 21

min 2nd | 22

dim 3rd | 23

(1) one CST smaller

(2) one CST larger

(3) smaller than a min 3rd

24  A min 3rd is (1) . . . . . . . . . than a maj 3rd. (Be precise.)
An aug 3rd is (2) . . . . . . . . . than a maj 3rd.
A dim 3rd is one CST (3) . . . . . . . . . .

two CST's smaller

25  A dim 6th is . . . . . . . . . than a maj 6th.

two CST's larger

26  An aug 2nd is . . . . . . . . . than a min 2nd.

(1)    (2)    (3)    (4)       (5)

42    Give the root and type of each triad.
Example: (1) C    maj

(2) C♭ maj
(3) C min
(4) E♭ maj
(5) E♯ min

(2) ___  _____
(3) ___  _____
(4) ___  _____
(5) ___  _____

43    Suppose A♯ is the *third*
of a major triad. Write
the complete triad:

44    Suppose A♭ is the third
of a minor triad. Write
the complete triad:

45    Suppose F is the fifth
of a major triad. Write
the complete triad:

46    Suppose E is the fifth
of a minor triad. Write
the complete triad:

Write the D major scale:

| 1 | |

The note lying a maj 6th above D is ___.

1) E

2) F#

3) C#

What note lies a maj 2nd above D? (1) ___

A maj 3rd above D is (2) ___.

A maj 7th above D is (3) ___.

major scale

To find major intervals above a given note, we refer to the _____  _____ built on the note.

Write the note which lies a maj 2nd above the given note:

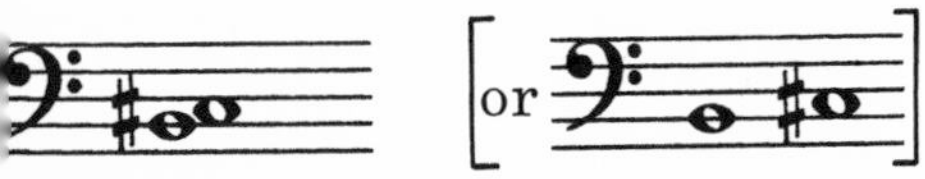

4

Construct a maj 2nd above the given note:

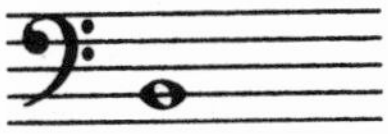

[or]

5

In naming and constructing intervals, always try to spell (silently or aloud) the needed scales. Write a scale (on scratch paper) only when necessary.

6

Construct a maj 3rd above the given note:

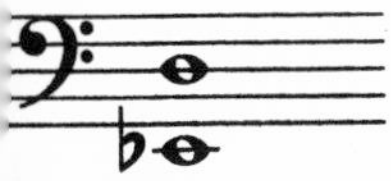

Construct a maj 7th above the given note:

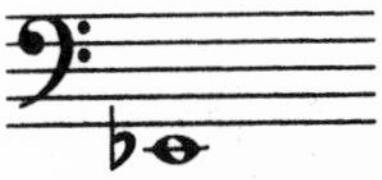

7

Label each triad maj or min:

(1) maj
(2) min
(3) min
(4) maj
(5) maj
(6) min

36

(1)___ (2)___ (3)___ (4)___    (5)___ (6)___

---

37  Construct a minor triad on the root F♯:

---

38  Construct a minor triad on the root A♭:

---

_minor triad with root D_

39  The expression _C major triad_ denotes a major triad with root C.  Similarly, the expression _D minor triad_ denotes a .......... .

---

40  Write an F maj  triad:

_(In all answers of this kind the entire chord may be written an octave higher or lower than shown.)_

---

41  Write a D♯ min triad:

---

1) contracted
2) CST

8

A maj 3rd (1) _____ (expanded *or* contracted) one (2) _____ makes a min 3rd.

---

9

Interval x shows a maj 6th above E. Construct interval y a min 6th above E:

---

10

Construct a min 3rd above the given note.
*(Hint: First find the maj 3rd above.)*

---

11

Construct a min 7th above the given note:

---

(1) expanded one

(2) contracted two

12

A maj interval must be (1) _____ _____ CST('s) to make an aug interval. A maj interval must be (2)_____ _____ CST('s) to make a dim interval.

---

13

Construct an aug 6th above the given note:

---

14

Construct a dim 7th above the given note:

---

tonic

15

The note on which a scale is built is the _____ .

---

# Set 19  The structure of triads (1)

(1) maj
(2) min
(3) min   (4) maj
(5) inverse

30  A major triad has a (1) _____ 3rd below a (2) _____ 3rd, while a minor triad has a (3) _____ 3rd below a (4) _____ 3rd. In structure, a minor triad is the (5) _____ of a major triad.

---

minor triad

31   This chord is a

_____  _____.

---

major triad

32 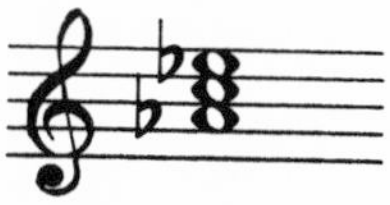  This chord is a

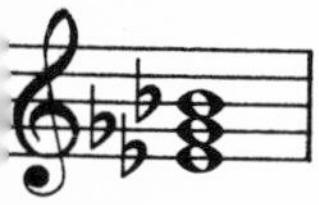

_____  _____.

---

33  A minor triad matches 1, 3 and 5, of a minor scale built on its root. Write the triad corresponding to 1, 3 and 5, of the E♭ minor scale:

minor

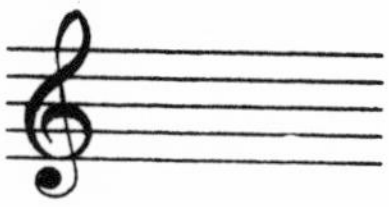

This is a _____ triad.

---

min

34 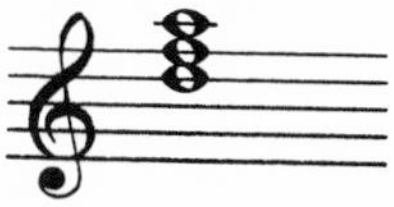  This is a _____ triad.

---

maj

35   This is a _____ triad.

---

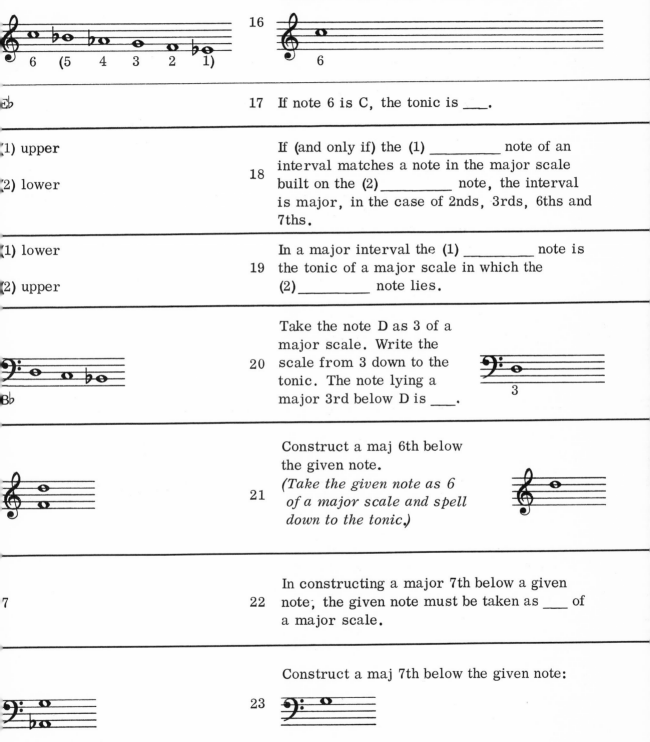

Take the note C as 6 of a major scale.
Write the scale from 6 *down* to the tonic:

16

6 (5  4  3  2  1)

6

E♭

17  If note 6 is C, the tonic is ___.

(1) upper

(2) lower

18  If (and only if) the (1) _____ note of an
interval matches a note in the major scale
built on the (2)_____ note, the interval
is major, in the case of 2nds, 3rds, 6ths and
7ths.

(1) lower

(2) upper

19  In a major interval the (1) _____ note is
the tonic of a major scale in which the
(2)_____ note lies.

B♭

20  Take the note D as 3 of a
major scale. Write the
scale from 3 down to the
tonic. The note lying a
major 3rd below D is ___.

3

21  Construct a maj 6th below
the given note.
*(Take the given note as 6
of a major scale and spell
down to the tonic.)*

7

22  In constructing a major 7th below a given
note, the given note must be taken as ___ of
a major scale.

23  Construct a maj 7th below the given note:

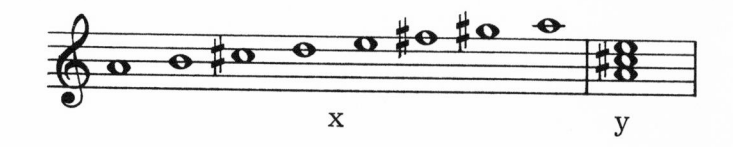

A major triad corresponds to 1, 3 and 5, of the major scale built on its root. Triad y matches. 1, 3 and 5, of scale x. Write the E♭ major scale and the triad formed by notes 1, 3 and 5:

27

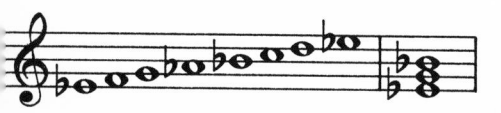

major

The triad thus formed is a _____ triad.

28

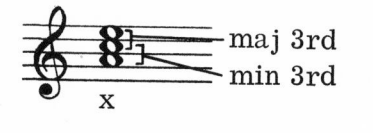

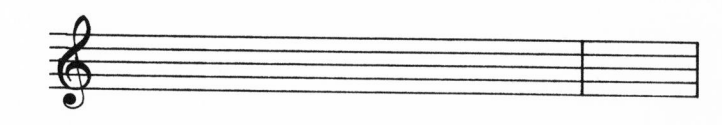

A triad composed of a minor 3rd below a major 3rd is a *minor triad*. Triad x is a minor triad.

(1) major

(2) minor

Triad y is a (1) _____ triad.
Triad z is a (2) _____ triad.

29

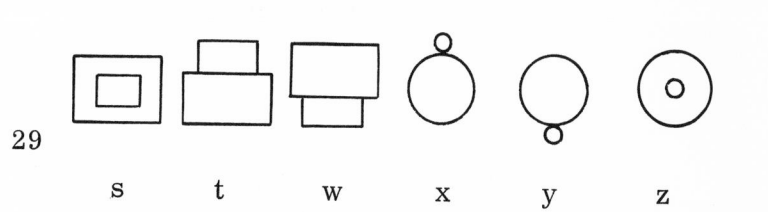

1) inverse   (2) x

Figure t is the inverse of figure w.
Figure y is the (1) _____ of figure (2)___.

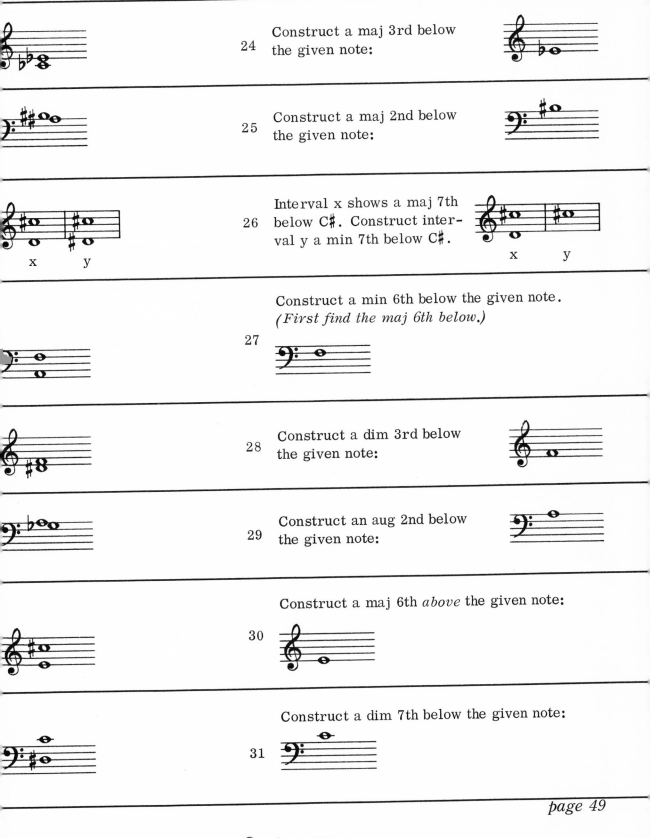

**24** Construct a maj 3rd below the given note:

**25** Construct a maj 2nd below the given note:

**26** Interval x shows a maj 7th below C♯. Construct interval y a min 7th below C♯.

x    y

**27** Construct a min 6th below the given note.
*(First find the maj 6th below.)*

**28** Construct a dim 3rd below the given note:

**29** Construct an aug 2nd below the given note:

**30** Construct a maj 6th *above* the given note:

**31** Construct a dim 7th below the given note:

major triad

21  A _____ _____ is composed of a
major 3rd below a minor third.

1) min
2) maj
3) is not

22  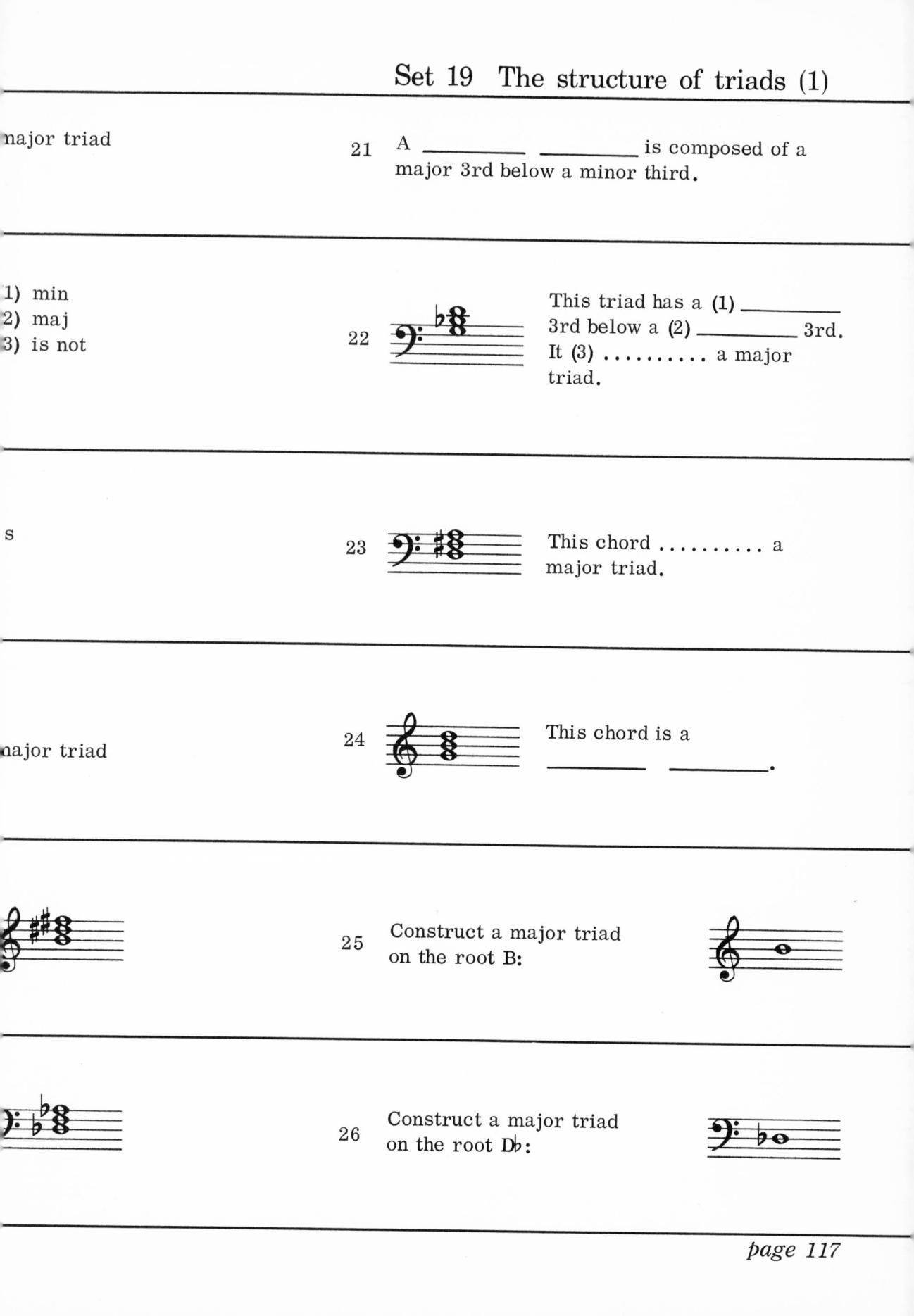 This triad has a (1) _____
3rd below a (2) _____ 3rd.
It (3) ......... a major
triad.

s

23  This chord ......... a
major triad.

major triad

24  This chord is a
_____ _____.

25  Construct a major triad
on the root B:

26  Construct a major triad
on the root Db:

relationship between
two pitches

1   An interval is the _____ _____ _____ _____.

(1) double
(2) general
(3) specific
*(2) and (3) in either order)*

2   Every interval has a (1) _____ name, consisting of a (2) _____ name and a (3) _____ name.

(1) prime
(2) octave
*(either order)*

3   Except for the names (1) _____ and (2) _____ , general names are ordinal numbers.

primes, 4ths,
5ths (and) octaves
*(any order)*

4   The specific names *major* and *minor* are used for 2nds, 3rds, 6ths and 7ths, *only*. They are not used for _____ , _____ , _____ and _____ .

major

5   In the case of 2nds, 3rds, 6ths and 7ths, if the upper note of the interval matches a note in the major scale built on the lower note, the specific name is _____ .

perfect

6   In the case of primes, 4ths, 5ths and octaves, if (and only if) the upper note matches a note in the major scale built on the lower note, the specific name is *perfect*. The given interval has the specific name _____ .

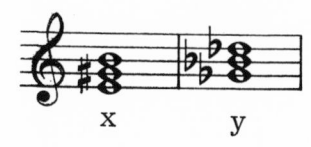

x        y

**17**  There are various structural types of triads, depending upon the specific names of the 3rds between the chord members. Both chord x and chord y have a major 3rd between root and third, and a minor 3rd between third and fifth. They are therefore .......... (the same *or* different) in structure.

the same

---

different

**18**     The two triads are ........ in structure.

---

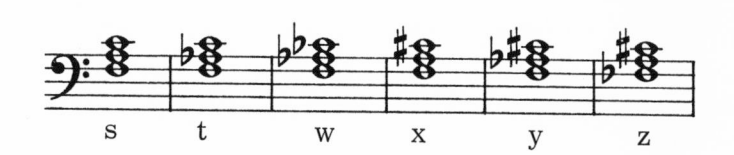

s        t        w        x        y        z

**19**

The triad structures of traditional harmony contain major and minor 3rds only. Which of the triads are *not* traditional harmonic structures? ..........

y and z

---

**20**

A triad composed of a major 3rd below a minor 3rd is a *major triad*. Chord x is a major triad. Chord y has a (1) _____ 3rd below a (2) _____ 3rd. It (3) .......... (is *or* is not) a major triad.

1) maj
2) min
3) is

7

erfect

The upper note of the interval matches a note in the major scale built on the lower note. Therefore, the specific name is _____ .

---

1) is not

2) is not

8

This interval (1) .........
(is or is not) perfect because the upper note (2) .........
(is or is not) in the major scale built on the lower note.

---

9

(1) will

(2) perfect

When two notes are identical, there is no upper or lower note, but, obviously, a scale constructed on either note (1) ......... (will or will not) contain the other note. Therefore, the interval is a (2) _____ prime.

---

is not

10

This interval ......... (is or is not) a perfect prime.

# Set 19  The structure of triads (1)

**(1) 3rd**

**(2) fifth**
**(3) 5th**
*(Except for this answer, do not consider it wrong if you give 3rd instead of third, or fifth instead of 5th, etc.)*

11  *3rd* and *5th* are general names of intervals. They also represent chord members. For clarity, this book uses *3rd* and *5th* for interval names, *third* and *fifth* for chord members. Thus the third lies a (1) _____ (3rd *or* third) above the root. The interval between between root and (2) _____ (5th *or* fifth?) is a (3) _____ (5th *or* fifth?).

---

12  Construct a triad on the root E. *(no sharps or flats)*

---

13  F is the *third* of a triad. Complete the triad. *(no sharps or flats)*

---

G

14  The fifth of a triad is D. Its root is ___. (Assume all notes are ♮.)

---

(1) major

(2) minor

15   In this triad the interval between root and third is a (1) _____ 3rd, and the interval between third and fifth is a (2) _____ 3rd.

---

(1) major 3rd

(2) minor 3rd

16   This triad has a (1) _____ _____ between root and third and a (2) _____ _____ between third and fifth.

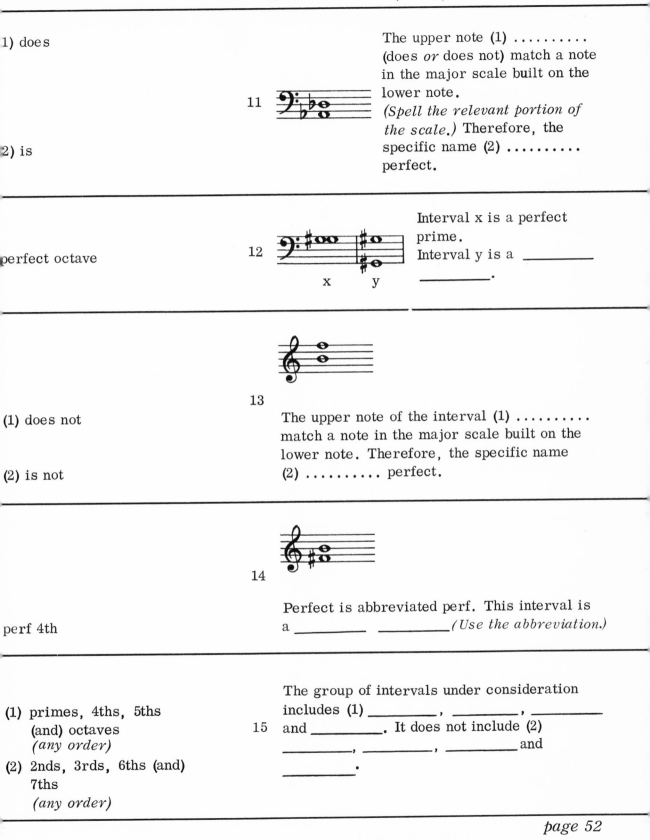

1) does

2) is

11

The upper note (1) .........
(does *or* does not) match a note
in the major scale built on the
lower note.
(*Spell the relevant portion of
the scale.*) Therefore, the
specific name (2) .........
perfect.

---

perfect octave

12

Interval x is a perfect
prime.
Interval y is a _____
_____.

        x        y

---

13

(1) does not

(2) is not

The upper note of the interval (1) .........
match a note in the major scale built on the
lower note. Therefore, the specific name
(2) ......... perfect.

---

14

perf 4th

Perfect is abbreviated perf. This interval is
a _____ _____ (*Use the abbreviation.*)

---

(1) primes, 4ths, 5ths
    (and) octaves
    *(any order)*

(2) 2nds, 3rds, 6ths (and)
    7ths
    *(any order)*

15

The group of intervals under consideration
includes (1) _____, _____, _____
and _____. It does not include (2)
_____, _____, _____ and
_____.

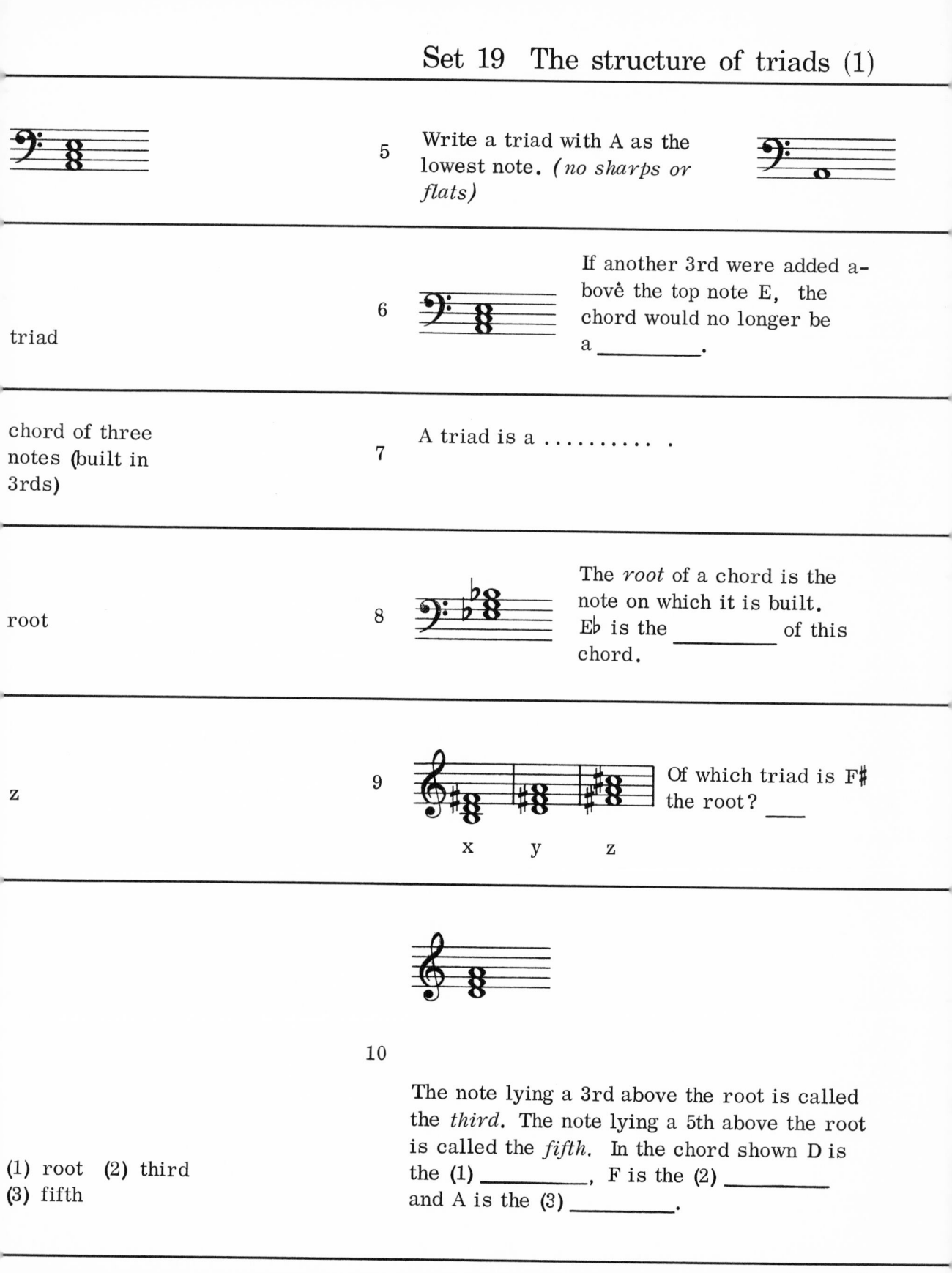

5    Write a triad with A as the lowest note. *( no sharps or flats)*

---

triad

6    If another 3rd were added a-bovè the top note E, the chord would no longer be a _____ .

---

chord of three notes (built in 3rds)

7    A triad is a ........... .

---

root

8    The *root* of a chord is the note on which it is built. E♭ is the _____ of this chord.

---

z

9    Of which triad is F♯ the root? ___

x    y    z

---

(1) root   (2) third
(3) fifth

10

The note lying a 3rd above the root is called the *third*. The note lying a 5th above the root is called the *fifth*. In the chord shown D is the (1) _____, F is the (2) _____ and A is the (3) _____ .

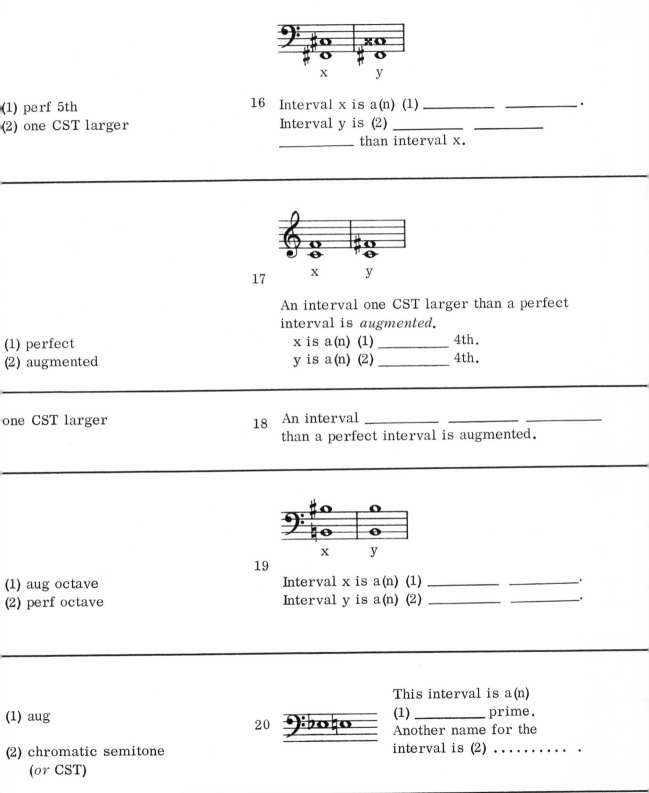

(1) perf 5th

(2) one CST larger

16  Interval x is a(n) (1) _____  _____ .
Interval y is (2) _____  _____
_____ than interval x.

(1) perfect

(2) augmented

17

An interval one CST larger than a perfect
interval is *augmented*.
x is a(n) (1) _____ 4th.
y is a(n) (2) _____ 4th.

one CST larger

18  An interval _____  _____  _____
than a perfect interval is augmented.

(1) aug octave

(2) perf octave

19

Interval x is a(n) (1) _____  _____ .
Interval y is a(n) (2) _____  _____ .

(1) aug

(2) chromatic semitone
(*or* CST)

20

This interval is a(n)
(1) _____ prime.
Another name for the
interval is (2) .......... .

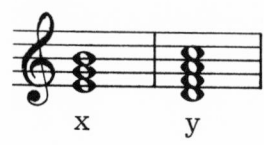

1 In traditional harmony chords are contructed in 3rds. Chord x has 3 notes and consists of these two 3rds:

3

Chord y has 4 notes and consists of ___ (how many?) 3rds.

2 Using C as the lowest note, construct a chord of five different notes. *(Do not use sharps or flats.)*

3rds

3 Chords are constructed in _____ .

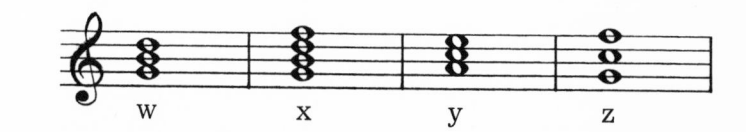

4

(1) y  (2) triad(s)

A chord of 3 notes built in 3rds is a *triad*. Chord w and chord (1) ___ are (2) _____ s.

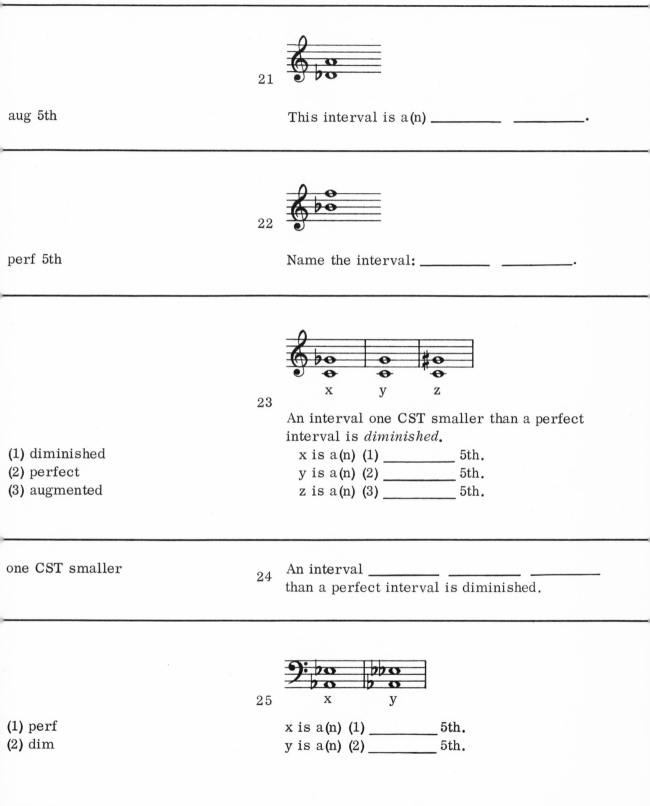

21

aug 5th

This interval is a(n) _____  _____.

22

perf 5th

Name the interval: _____  _____.

23

(1) diminished
(2) perfect
(3) augmented

An interval one CST smaller than a perfect
interval is *diminished*.
x is a(n) (1) _____ 5th.
y is a(n) (2) _____ 5th.
z is a(n) (3) _____ 5th.

one CST smaller

24  An interval _____ _____ _____
than a perfect interval is diminished.

25

(1) perf
(2) dim

x is a(n) (1) _____ 5th.
y is a(n) (2) _____ 5th.

**Step 3.** Now let's return to the series of 5ths *up* from C. Recite this series as a series of *major keys*, giving the signature of each key as you go along, like this:

no sharps or flats  C      one sharp  G      two sharps  D...
.......... and so on to ......... seven sharps  C♯

**Step 4.** Recite the series of 5ths *down* from C as a series of major keys with signatures:

no sharps or flats  C       one flat  F       two flats  B♭ ....
.......... and so on to ......... seven flats  C♭

**Step 5.** Cover the bottom row of the following table with the masking card. Name aloud the major key corresponding to the first given signature (3♯). Expose the first member of the bottom row to check your answer. Complete the entire table in this way, checking each item as you go along. Then cover the *top* row and give the signatures for the major keys, one at a time. Go through the table backwards as well as forwards. Repeat these operations until speed and assurance are felt. At first you will get most of your answers by going through the series of keys, as practiced above. The more you practice, the more often you will be able to answer without the help of the series.

| 3♯ | 5♭ | 6♯ | 7♭ | 1♯ | 4♭ | 4♯ | 1♭ | 7♯ | 6♭ | 5♯ | 3♭ | 2♯ | 2♭ | 4♯ | 7♭ | 2♯ | 3♭ | 6♯ | 5♭ | 1♯ | 1♭ | 5♯ | 6♭ | 3♯ | 2♭ | 7♯ | 4♭ |
|---|---|---|---|---|---|---|---|---|---|---|---|---|---|---|---|---|---|---|---|---|---|---|---|---|---|---|---|
| A | D♭ | F♯ | C♭ | G | A♭ | E | F | C♯ | G♭ | B | E♭ | D | B♭ | E | C♭ | D | E♭ | F♯ | D♭ | G | F | B | G♭ | A | B♭ | C♯ | A♭ |

**Step 6.** The table below contains minor keys (symbolized by small letters) and their signatures. Practice as above. At first, you will rely mostly on association with the relative major keys. The more you practice, the more readily your responses will come without thinking of the relative major key.

| 1♯ | 5♭ | 3♯ | 4♭ | 7♯ | 1♭ | 6♯ | 3♭ | 2♯ | 7♭ | 5♯ | 6♭ | 4♯ | 2♭ | 7♯ | 5♭ | 4♯ | 4♭ | 6♯ | 2♭ | 1♯ | 7♭ | 5♯ | 3♭ | 3♯ | 6♭ | 2♯ | 1♭ |
|---|---|---|---|---|---|---|---|---|---|---|---|---|---|---|---|---|---|---|---|---|---|---|---|---|---|---|---|
| e | b♭ | f♯ | f | a♯ | d | d♯ | c | b | a♭ | g♯ | e♭ | c♯ | g | a♯ | b♭ | c♯ | f | d♯ | g | e | a♭ | g♯ | c | f♯ | e♭ | b | d |

Now place the masking card as usual and go on to the next set.

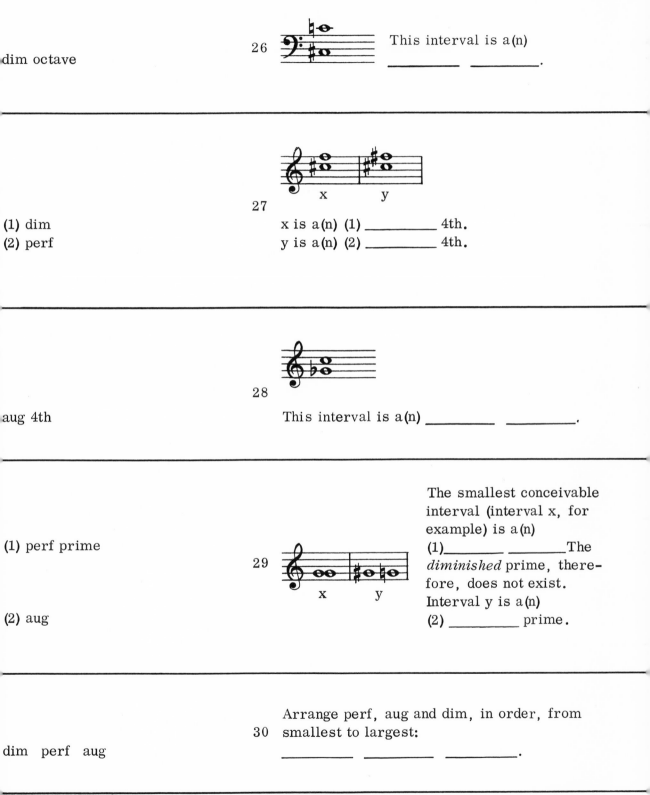

dim octave

26    This interval is a(n)

_____ _____.

---

27

**(1) dim**
**(2) perf**

x is a(n) (1) _____ 4th.
y is a(n) (2) _____ 4th.

---

28

aug 4th

This interval is a(n) _____ _____.

---

**(1) perf prime**

29

The smallest conceivable interval (interval x, for example) is a(n)
(1)_____ _____The *diminished* prime, there-fore, does not exist.
Interval y is a(n)

**(2) aug**

(2) _____ prime.

---

30   Arrange perf, aug and dim, in order, from smallest to largest:

dim  perf  aug

_____ _____ _____.

30  Write the signature of
G♯ minor:

Write the scale of the relative major of C♯
minor, with key signature:

31

Write the F harmonic minor scale, with key
signature:

32

33  Remove the masking card and read below.

The following will show you how to practice for greater speed in associating keys and their signatures. Six steps are given. *Practice each step and master it before going on to the next step.*

Step 1.  Given below is the series of 5ths up from C, stopping at C♯. Cover the series with the masking card and practice reciting it aloud. At first, uncover one member of the series at a time to check you recitation. Later, try to recite the whole series, stopping to check only when you are not sure of what follows.

C    G    D    A    E    B    F♯    C♯

Step 2.  Practice the series *down* from C in the same way.

C    F    B♭    E♭    A♭    D♭    G♭    C♭

Name the following intervals:

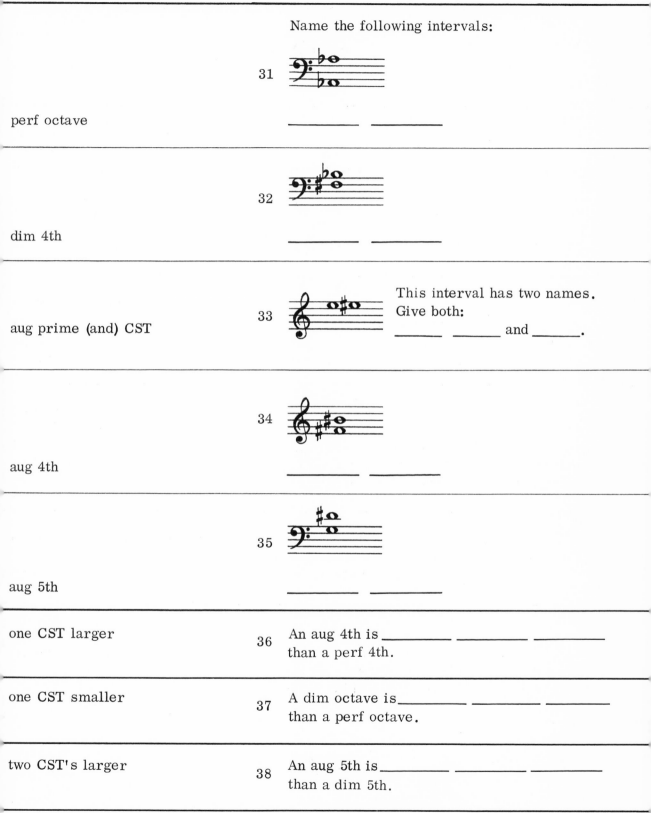

31

perf octave

_____  _____

32

dim 4th

_____  _____

33

This interval has two names.
Give both:
_____ _____ and _____.

aug prime (and) CST

34

aug 4th

_____  _____

35

aug 5th

_____  _____

one CST larger

36  An aug 4th is _____ _____ _____
than a perf 4th.

one CST smaller

37  A dim octave is _____ _____ _____
than a perf octave.

two CST's larger

38  An aug 5th is _____ _____ _____
than a dim 5th.

*page 56*

23

(1) sharp    (2) C
(3) accidentals

Signs not belonging to the key signature are
called *accidentals.* In this example the natural
before B and the (1) _____ before (2) ___
are (3) _____ .

---

(1) major

(2) melodic (minor) descending

24

Major key signatures correspond to (1)........
scales. Minor key signatures correspond to
(2) ........ scales.

---

(1) major
(2) signs
(3) major key
(4) (key) signature

25

For every melodic minor descending scale
there is a (1) ........ scale with the same
(2) .......... . Therefore, for every minor
key there is a (3) ........ with the same
(4) ........ .

---

(1) major
(2) minor 3rd
(3) minor
(4) (key) signature

26

If the tonic of a (1) ........ key lies a
(2) ........ above the tonic of a (3) ........
key, the two keys have the same (4) ......... .

---

the same signature

27

Two keys that have .......... are relative
keys.

---

melodic minor
ascending and
harmonic minor

28

Which scales require accidentals when written
with the key signature? ..........

---

Bb

29

What minor key has this
signature? ___

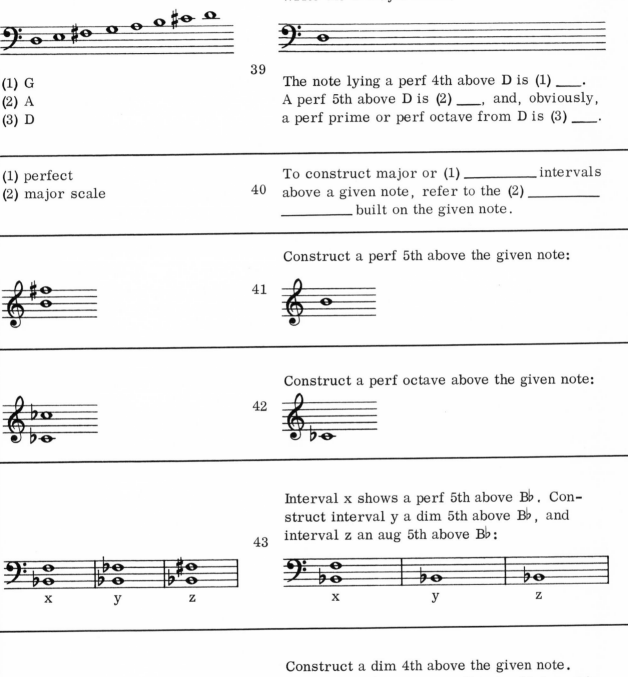

Write the D major scale:

39

The note lying a perf 4th above D is (1) ___.
A perf 5th above D is (2) ___, and, obviously,
a perf prime or perf octave from D is (3) ___.

(1) G
(2) A
(3) D

(1) perfect
(2) major scale

40

To construct major or (1) _____ intervals
above a given note, refer to the (2) _____
_____ built on the given note.

Construct a perf 5th above the given note:

41

Construct a perf octave above the given note:

42

Interval x shows a perf 5th above B♭. Construct interval y a dim 5th above B♭, and
interval z an aug 5th above B♭:

43

x          y          z

Construct a dim 4th above the given note.
*(First find the corresponding perf interval.)*

44

melodic (minor) descending

**18**  Minor key signatures correspond to .......... scales.

**19**  Write the B melodic minor descending scale preceded by its key signature:

(1) do not

(2) do not

**20**  Minor key signatures (1) .......... (do *or* do not) correspond to melodic minor ascending scales. Minor key signatures (2) .......... correspond to harmonic minor scales.

**21**  When melodic minor ascending scales or harmonic minor scales are written with their key signatures, one or two signs must be inserted before the notes of the scale. Write the E♭ melodic minor ascending scale, first without the key signature, then with the key signature. Check carefully to see that the two scales are identical.

**22**  Write the F♯ harmonic minor scale, first without the key signature, then with the key signature:

write signature

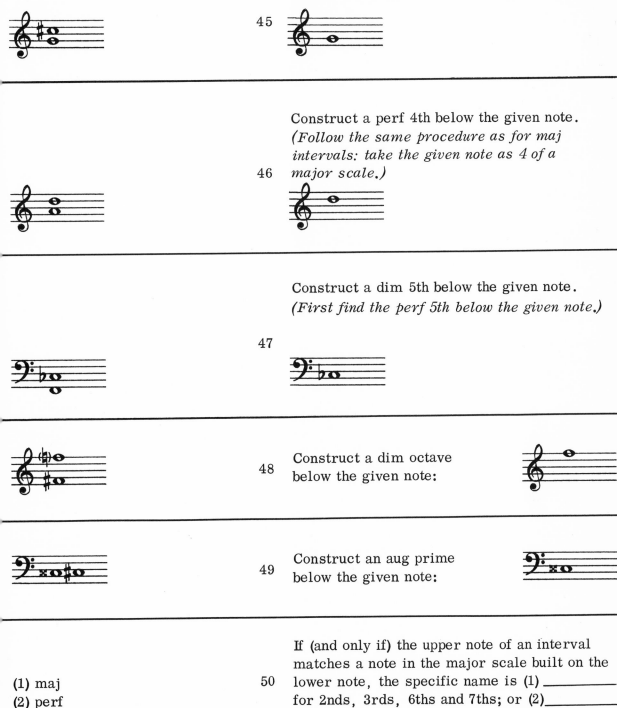

**45** Construct an aug 4th above the given note:

**46** Construct a perf 4th below the given note. *(Follow the same procedure as for maj intervals: take the given note as 4 of a major scale.)*

**47** Construct a dim 5th below the given note. *(First find the perf 5th below the given note.)*

**48** Construct a dim octave below the given note:

**49** Construct an aug prime below the given note:

**50** If (and only if) the upper note of an interval matches a note in the major scale built on the lower note, the specific name is (1) _____ for 2nds, 3rds, 6ths and 7ths; or (2)_____ for primes, 4ths, 5ths and octaves.

(1) maj
(2) perf

# Set 18  Minor key signatures (2)

D♯ (minor) *(The relative minor of F♯ major)*

11  What minor key has a signature of 6 sharps? ___
*(First find the major key with 6 sharps.)*

A♭

12  What minor key has a signature of 7 flats?

F♯

13  3 sharps is the signature of ___ minor.

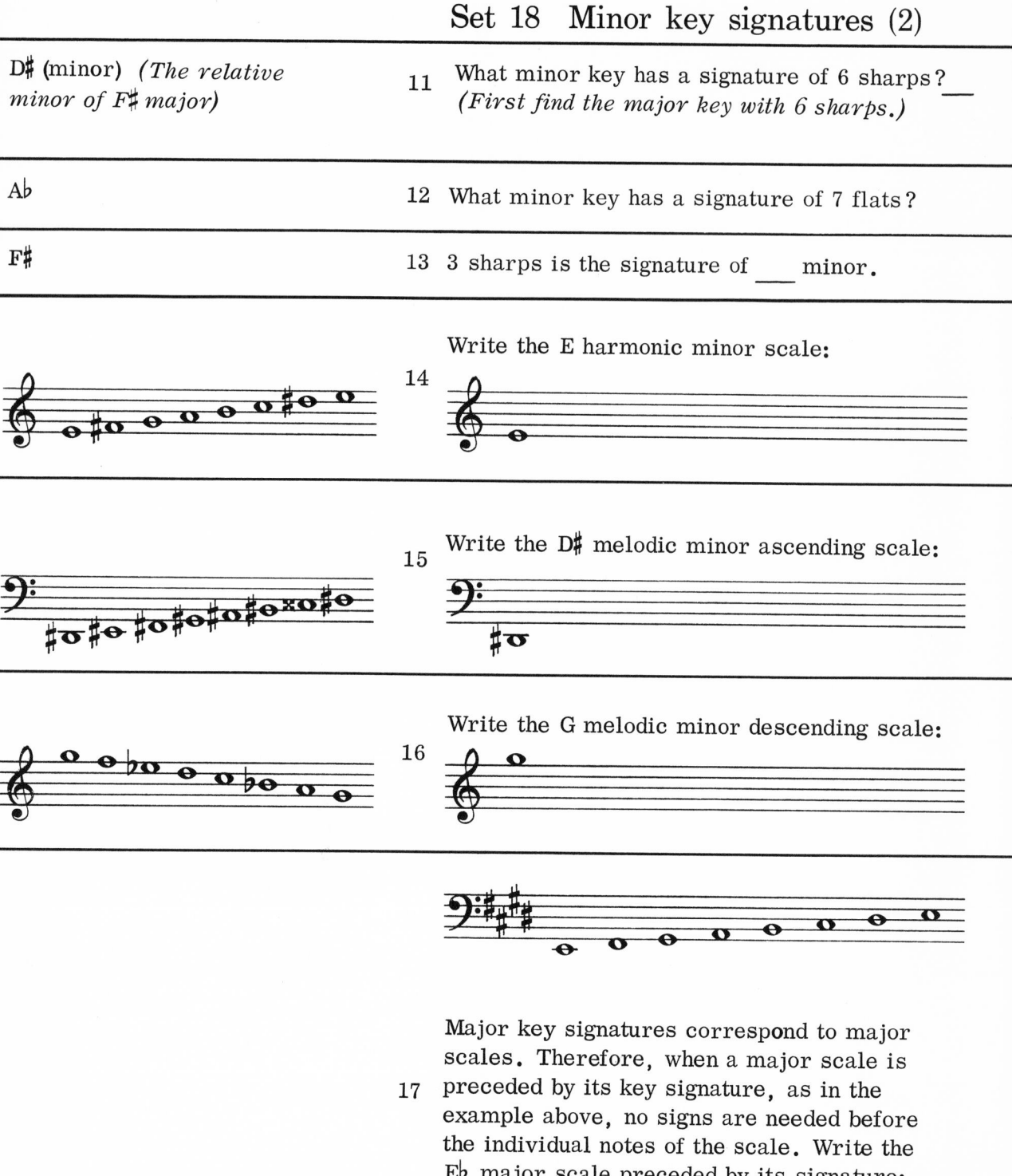

14  Write the E harmonic minor scale:

15  Write the D♯ melodic minor ascending scale:

16  Write the G melodic minor descending scale:

17  Major key signatures correspond to major scales. Therefore, when a major scale is preceded by its key signature, as in the example above, no signs are needed before the individual notes of the scale. Write the E♭ major scale preceded by its signature:

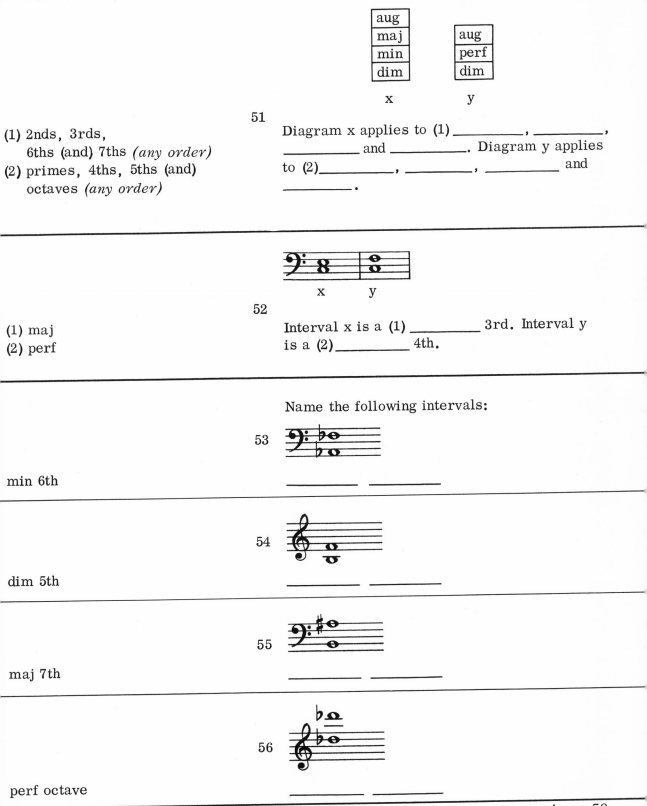

| aug |
| maj |
| min |
| dim |
x

| aug |
| perf |
| dim |
y

51

(1) 2nds, 3rds,
6ths (and) 7ths *(any order)*
(2) primes, 4ths, 5ths (and)
octaves *(any order)*

Diagram x applies to (1) _____ , _____ ,
_____ and _____ . Diagram y applies
to (2) _____ , _____ , _____ and
_____ .

52

(1) maj
(2) perf

Interval x is a (1) _____ 3rd. Interval y
is a (2) _____ 4th.

Name the following intervals:

53

min 6th

_____   _____

54

dim 5th

_____   _____

55

maj 7th

_____   _____

56

perf octave

_____   _____

|  |  |  |
|---|---|---|
| (1) signature  (2) relative | 1 | Two keys having the same signature are called *relative* keys. E♭ major and C minor have the same (1) _____. They are (2) _____ keys. |
| G minor | 2 | The terms *relative minor* and *relative major* are applied in this way: C minor is the relative minor of E♭ major. E♭ major is the relative major of C minor. The relative minor of B♭ major is ___ _____. |
| relative major | 3 | C major is the _____ _____ of A minor. |
| D major | 4 | The relative major of B minor is ___ _____. |
| (1) relative major<br>(2) 2 sharps<br>(3) 2 sharps | 5 | D major, the (1) .......... of B minor, has a signature of (2) ___ _____. The signature of B minor is (3) ___ _____. |
| 4 sharps *(same as E major)* | 6 | The signature of C♯ minor is ___ _____. (*First find the relative major and its signature.*) |
| 1 flat | 7 | The signature of D minor is ___ _____. |
| 5 sharps | 8 | G♯ minor has a signature of ___ _____. |
| | 9 | Write the signature of A♯ minor: |
| | 10 | Write the signature of E♭ minor: |

# Set 10 Doubly diminished and augmented intervals

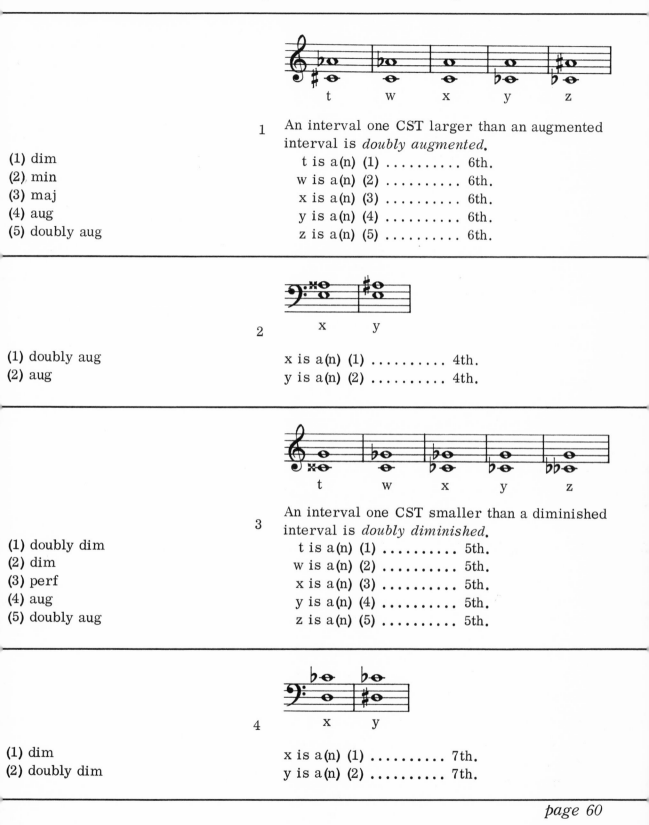

**1** An interval one CST larger than an augmented interval is *doubly augmented.*

(1) dim        t is a(n) (1) .......... 6th.
(2) min       w is a(n) (2) .......... 6th.
(3) maj       x is a(n) (3) .......... 6th.
(4) aug       y is a(n) (4) .......... 6th.
(5) doubly aug     z is a(n) (5) .......... 6th.

**2**

(1) doubly aug     x is a(n) (1) .......... 4th.
(2) aug        y is a(n) (2) .......... 4th.

**3** An interval one CST smaller than a diminished interval is *doubly diminished.*

(1) doubly dim     t is a(n) (1) .......... 5th.
(2) dim        w is a(n) (2) .......... 5th.
(3) perf       x is a(n) (3) .......... 5th.
(4) aug        y is a(n) (4) .......... 5th.
(5) doubly aug    z is a(n) (5) .......... 5th.

**4**

(1) dim         x is a(n) (1) .......... 7th.
(2) doubly dim    y is a(n) (2) .......... 7th.

# Set 17   Minor key signatures (1)

| | | |
|---|---|---|
| D | 17 | The tonics of two keys represented by the same signature are always a minor 3rd apart. The *major* tonic is the *higher* of the two. F major and ____ minor have the same signature. |
| (1) C♯ <br> (2) 4 sharps | 18 | E major and (1) ____ minor have the same signature, which is (2) ____ _____. |
| (1) min 3rd <br> (2) above | 19 | If two keys have the same signature the major tonic lies a(n) (1) _____ _____. <br> (2) _____ (above *or* below) the minor tonic. |
| (1) B♭ <br> (2) 2 flats | 20 | (1) ____ major and G minor have the same signature, namely (2) ____ _____. |
| 5 flats | 21 | B♭ minor has a signature of ____ _____. <br> *(First find the major key with the same signature.)* |
| no sharps or flats | 22 | The signature of A minor is.......... . |
| (1) major   (2) min 3rd <br> (3) minor | 23 | Two keys have the same signature when the (1) _____ tonic lies a (2) _____ _____ above the (3) _____ tonic. |

Complete this table:

24

| signature | 7♭'s | 6♭'s | 5♭'s | 4♭'s | 3♭'s | 2♭'s | 1♭ | no |
|---|---|---|---|---|---|---|---|---|
| major key | __ | __ | D♭ | __ | E♭ | __ | __ | C |
| minor key | __ | __ | B♭ | __ | C | __ | __ | A |

Answers: C♭ G♭ (D♭) A♭ (E♭) B♭ F (C)  /  A♭ E♭ (B♭) F (C) G D (A)

| signature | 1♯ | 2♯'s | 3♯'s | 4♯'s | 5♯'s | 6♯'s | 7♯'s |
|---|---|---|---|---|---|---|---|
| major key | G | __ | __ | __ | __ | __ | __ |
| minor key | E | __ | __ | __ | __ | __ | __ |

Answers: (G) D A E B F♯ C♯  /  (E) B F♯ C♯ G♯ D♯ A♯

| | | |
|---|---|---|
| two CST's larger | 5 | A doubly aug 6th is ＿＿＿＿ ＿＿＿＿ ＿＿＿＿ than a maj 6th. |

| | | |
|---|---|---|
| two CST's smaller | 6 | A doubly dim 4th is ＿＿＿＿ ＿＿＿＿ ＿＿＿＿ than a perf 4th. |

doubly aug 3rd

7   Name the interval .........

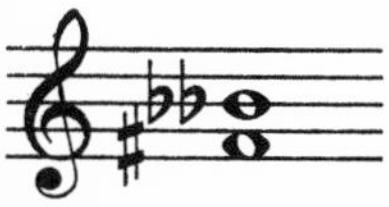

Construct a doubly dim 4th above the given note:

8

Construct a doubly dim 5th below the given note:

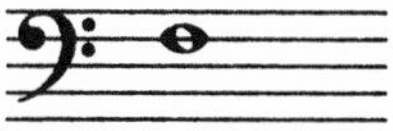

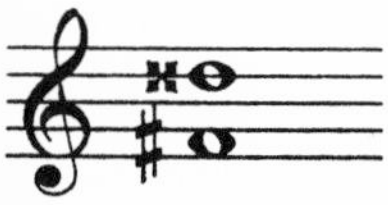

9

Construct an aug 6th below the given note:

10

If both notes of an interval are raised (or lowered) one CST, the size of the interval

is not

11  ......... (is *or* is not) changed.

(1) G

(2) E

12   For every melodic minor descending scale there is a major scale having the same signs. Therefore, each key signature is used for one minor key and one major key. The given signature stands for (1) ___ major or (2) ___ minor.

(1) (key) signature
(2) major
(3) minor
*((2) and (3) in either order.)*

13   Each (1) ......... represents one (2) _____ key and one (3) _____ key.

min 3rd

14   As previously shown E♭ major and C minor have the same signature. C and E♭ form a(n) ......... . *(Name the interval.)*

min 3rd

15   G major and E minor have the same signature. E and G are a(n) ......... apart.

(1) C

(2) min 3rd

16   This "signature" (no sharps or flats) represents either the key of A minor or the key of (1) ___ major. Again, the interval between the two tonics is a(n) (2) ......... .

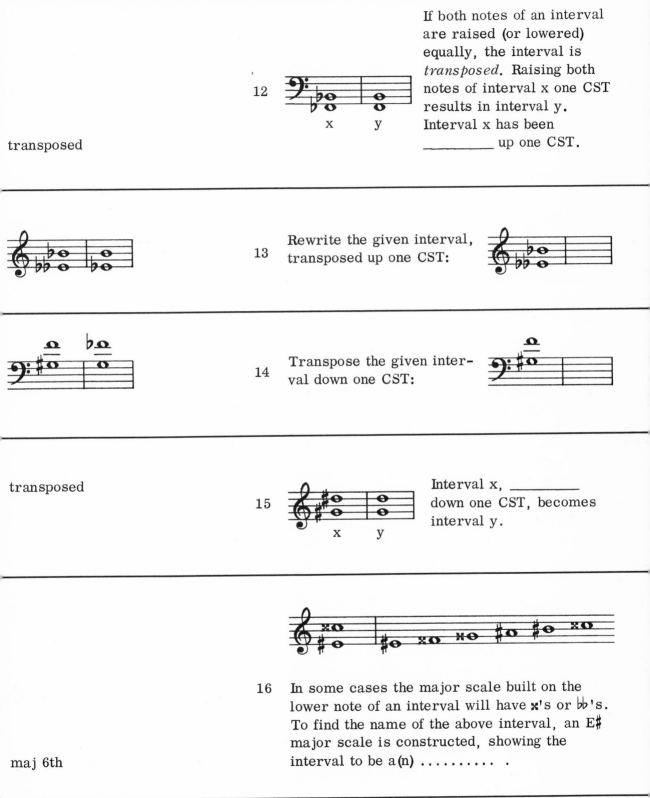

**12**

If both notes of an interval are raised (or lowered) equally, the interval is *transposed*. Raising both notes of interval x one CST results in interval y. Interval x has been _____ up one CST.

transposed

**13**  Rewrite the given interval, transposed up one CST:

**14**  Transpose the given interval down one CST:

transposed

**15**  Interval x, _____ down one CST, becomes interval y.

**16**  In some cases the major scale built on the lower note of an interval will have ×'s or ♭♭'s. To find the name of the above interval, an E♯ major scale is constructed, showing the interval to be a(n) ......... .

maj 6th

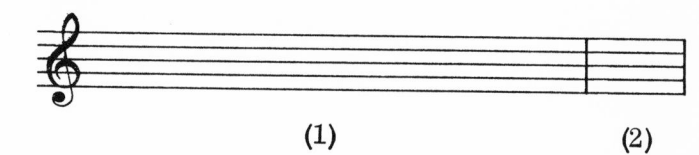

# Set 17 Minor key signatures (1)

8 (1) Write the scale to which the key signature of F♯ minor corresponds.

(2) Write the signature of F♯ minor.

(1) (2)

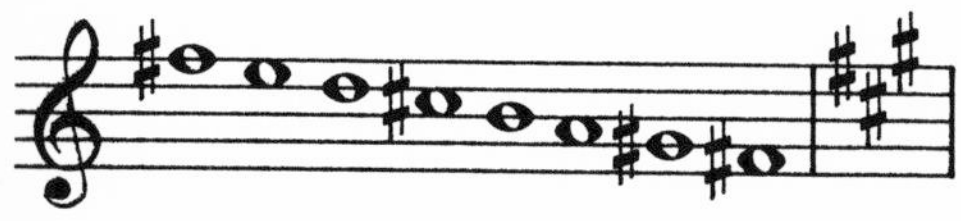

*(The scale really has only 3 sharps, not 4; hence the signature is 3 sharps.)*

---

9

E♭ major C melodic minor descending

The E♭ major scale and the C melodic minor descending scale both contain E♭, A♭ and B♭, other notes being ♮. These two scales have the same __________.

signs (*or* flats)

---

10 Since the scales of E♭ major and C melodic minor descending have the same signs, the two keys of E♭ and C minor have the same key __________.

signature

---

11 Write the indicated scales:

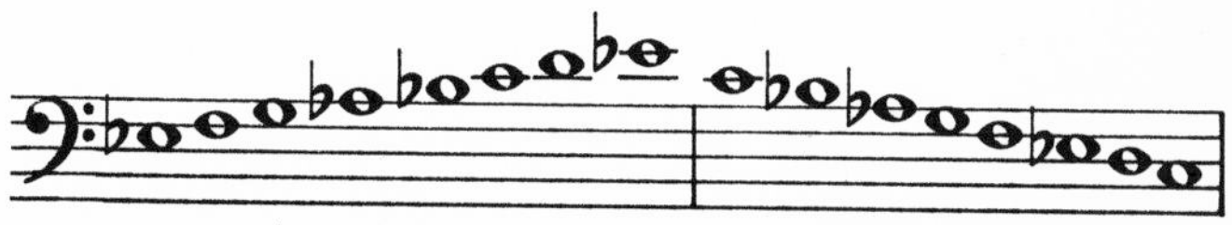

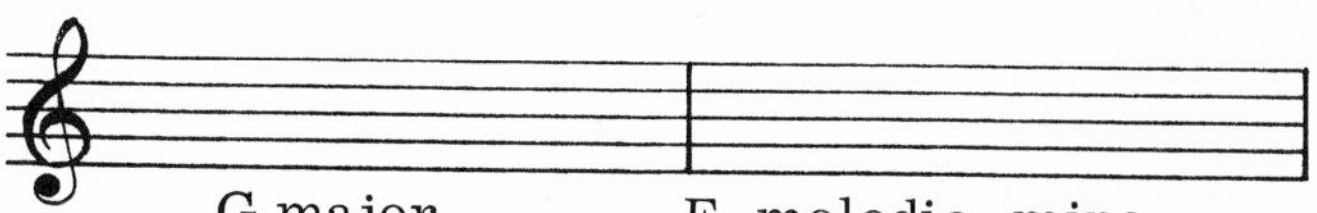

G major E melodic minor descending

The two scales have the same (1) ........... Therefore, the keys of G major and E minor have the same (2) ..........., which is (3) ___ __________.

(1) sign(s)

(2) (key) signature

(3) 1 sharp

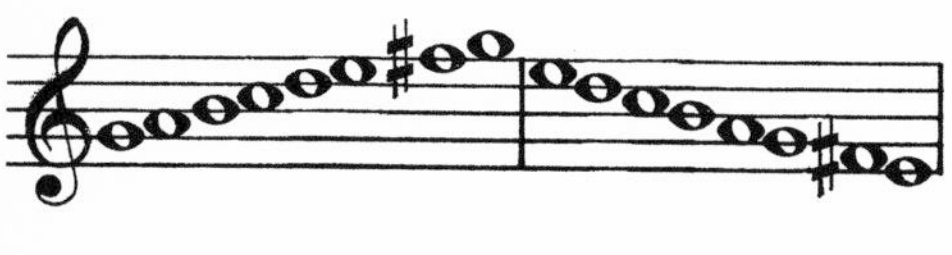

When the lower note of an interval supports a
major scale with ✗'s or ♭♭'s, it is simpler to
measure a transposition of the interval than
the interval itself. Show how the given interval
17  might be transposed for more convenient
measurement:

maj 6th

18

This interval is a(n) .......... .
*(Mentally transpose the interval up one CST.)*

Name the following intervals:

19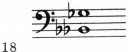

dim 7th

.........

20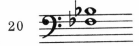

aug 4th

.........

21

aug 6th

.........

| | | |
|---|---|---|
| signs (*or* sharps) | 1 | The scale of D major and the key signature of D major have the same _____ . |
| D major | 2 | Another way of stating the same thing is: The key signature of D major corresponds to the ___ _____ scale. |
| melodic minor descending | 3 | The minor key signatures correspond to the *melodic minor descending* scale. Thus, the key signature of B minor contains the same signs as the B _____ _____ _____ scale. |

4

| | | |
|---|---|---|
| (1) 4 <br> (2) 4 flats | | The descending melodic minor scale of F has (1) ___ flats. The key signature of F minor is (2) ____ _____ . |
| (key) signature | 5 | The G melodic minor descending scale has the same signs as the ......... of G minor. |
| (1) major <br><br> (2) melodic (minor) descending | 6 | Major key signatures correspond to (1) ....... scales. Minor key signatures correspond to (2) ......... scales. |

7

Write the C melodic minor descending scale:

3 flats

The key signature of C minor is ___ _____ .

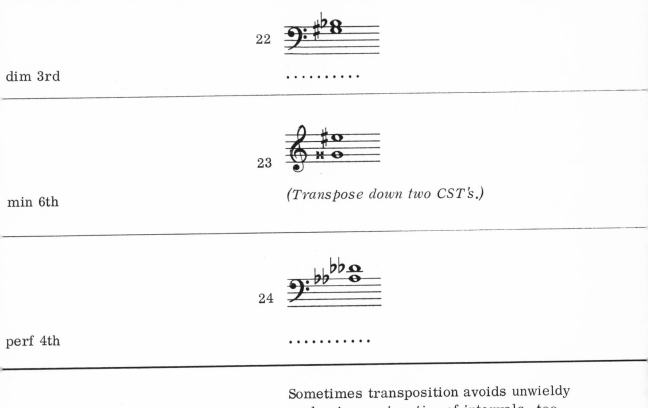

dim 3rd

22

..........

min 6th

23

*(Transpose down two CST's.)*

perf 4th

24

..........

Sometimes transposition avoids unwieldy scales in *construction* of intervals, too. Construct a maj 6th above the given note, B♯, in this way: First construct a maj 6th above B, then transpose up one CST.

25

Construct a dim 5th below the given note:

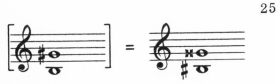

26

*(To avoid complications, construct from B♭, then transpose.)*

# Set 16  Minor scales

| | | |
|---|---|---|
| 2–3 | 33 | All forms of the minor scale have a DST at ___. |
| 3 | 34 | The harmonic minor scale has ___ (*how many?*) DST locations. |
| (1) 2–3<br>(2) 5–6<br>(3) 7–8<br>(4) aug 2nd<br>(5) 6–7 | 35 | The harmonic minor scale has DST's at (1)___, (2)___ and (3)___, a(n) (4)_____ _____ at (5)___, and whole tones everywhere else. |
| (1) 2–3 (and) 7–8<br>(2) 2–3 (and) 5–6 | 36 | The melodic minor ascending scale has DST's at (1)___ and ___. The melodic minor descending scale has DST's at (2)___ and ___. |
| F♯ G♯ A B C♯ D E♯ F♯ | 37 | Spell the F♯ harmonic minor scale:<br> F♯ __ __ __ __ __ __ F♯ |
| D♯ E♯ F♯ G♯ A♯ B♯ C𝄪 D♯ | 38 | Spell the D♯ melodic minor ascending scale:<br> D♯ __ __ __ __ __ __ D♯ |
| F E♭ D♭ C B♭ A♭ G F | 39 | Spell the F melodic minor descending scale:<br> F __ __ __ __ __ __ F |

Certain minor scales require one or two double sharps. Write the indicated scales:

40

G♯ harmonic minor

41

A♯ melodic minor ascending

Intervals with general names not larger than "octave" are *simple* intervals. Intervals with general names larger than "octave" are *compound* intervals. Label each of these intervals simple or compound:

1

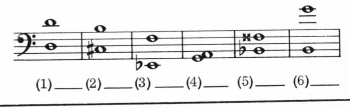

(1) ___ (2) ___ (3) ___ (4) ___ (5) ___ (6) ___

(1) simple    (2) simple
(3) compound  (4) simple
(5) simple    (6) compound

---

2  The general name of a compound interval is found in the usual way, by counting the lines and spaces from one note to the other, inclusively. The general name of the given interval is _____ .

10th

---

3  Give the general names:

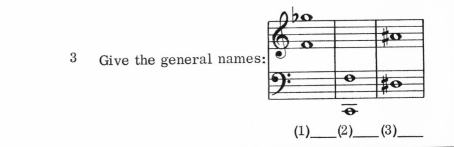

(1) ___ (2) ___ (3) ___

(1) 9th
(2) 11th
(3) 12th

---

To find the specific name of a compound interval, reduce it to a simple interval by subtracting one or more octaves. Subtracting an octave from interval x results in interval y. Write the interval which results when an octave is subtracted from interval z:

4

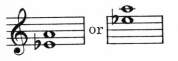

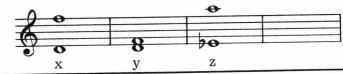

x       y       z

# Set 16 Minor scales

7-8

**25** The melodic minor ascending has DST's at 2-3 and ___.

5-6

**26** The melodic minor descending has DST's at 2-3 and ___.

whole tones

**27** The melodic minor scales, like the major scales, consist entirely of DST's and ........

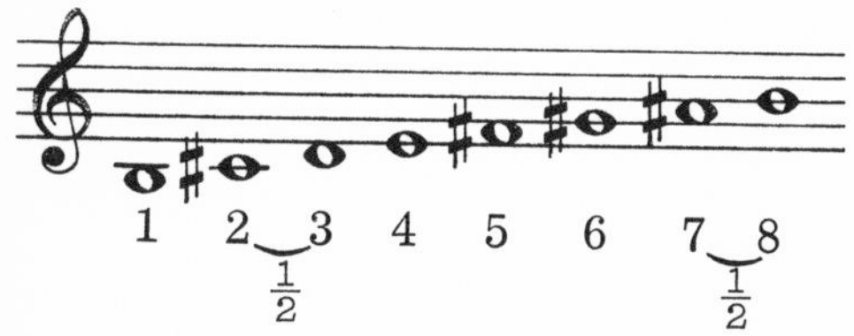

**28** Write the B melodic minor ascending scale. Mark the DST locations first.

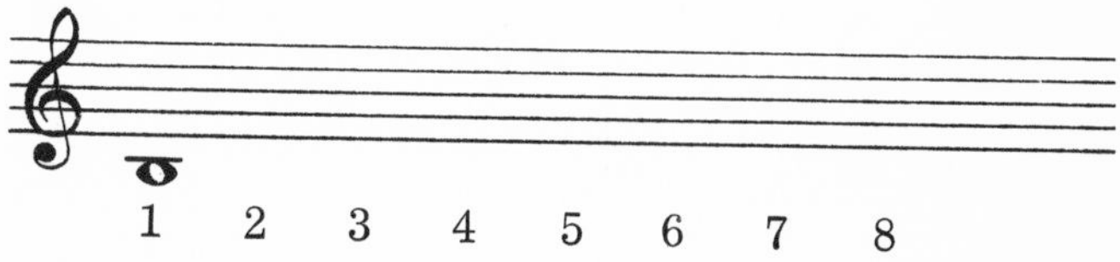

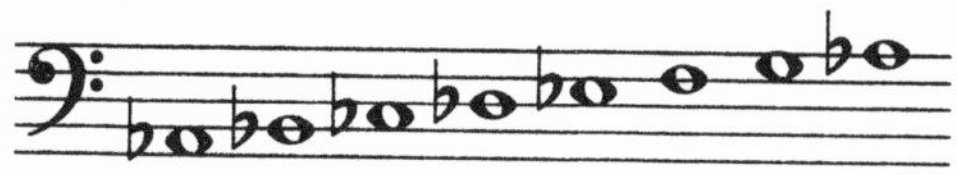

**29** Write the A♭ melodic minor ascending scale:

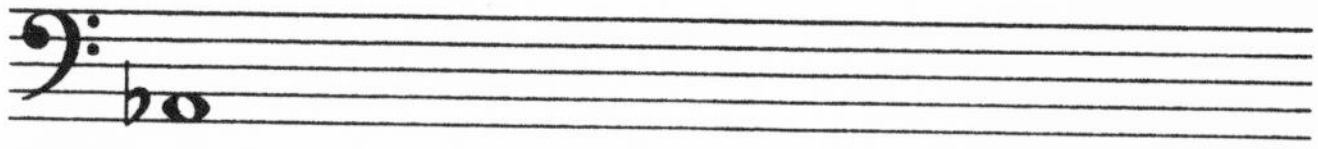

2-3 (and) 5-6

**30** The melodic minor descending has DST's at ___ and ___.

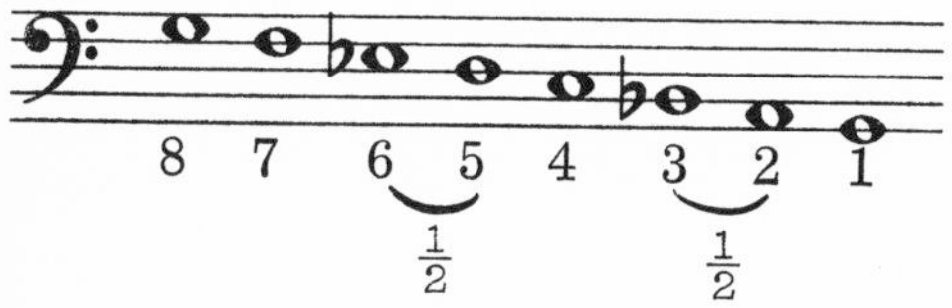

**31** Write the G melodic minor descending scale. Mark the DST locations first.

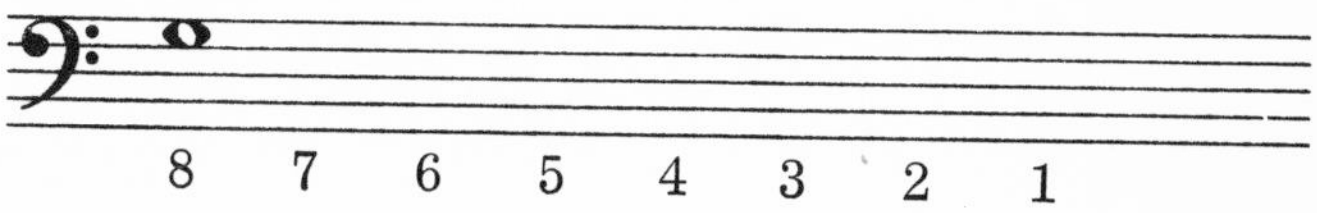

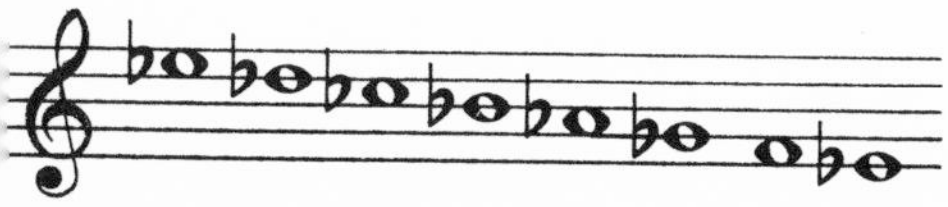

**32** Write the E♭ melodic minor descending scale:

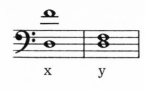

x      y

5

A compound interval has the same specific
name as the corresponding simple interval.
Interval x has the same specific name as
interval y. The specific name is _____.

min

6

This interval has the specific name _____.

aug

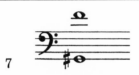

7

The specific name of this interval is _____.

dim

Sometimes more than one octave must be subtracted from the interval in order to reduce it
to a simple interval. Subtract two octaves
from the given interval:

8

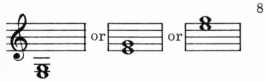

The specific name is _____.

min

9

Name the interval: .........

maj 10th

# Set 16   Minor scales

*ascending*        *descending*

20        C  melodic  minor  scales

descending

Two other forms of the minor scale are the *melodic minor ascending*, and the *melodic minor _____*.

---

(1) DST's
(2) aug 2nd(s)

21   As the examples in frame 20 show, the melodic minor scales consist entirely of whole tones and (1) .......... . Unlike the harmonic minor scale, they contain no (2) ..........

---

(1) 1   (2) 5
(3) 2-3

22   All minor scales have the same structure from note (1) ___ to note (2) ___, including a DST at (3) ___.

---

1 2  3 4 5 6 7 8    8 7   6 5 4  3  2 1

23

(1) 7-8
(2) 5-6

The melodic minor ascending has DST's at 2-3 and (1) ___. The melodic minor descending has DST's at 2-3 and (2) ___.

---

(1) ascending
(2) descending

24   The location of the DST's in the melodic minor scales causes notes 6 and 7 to be higher in the melodic minor (1) _____ than in the melodic minor (2)_____.

---

10

ug 13th

Name the interval: .........

---

11  A 9th reduced by an octave becomes a 2nd.
A 10th reduced by an octave becomes a
_____.

3rd

---

12  The simple interval corresponding to an 11th
is a 4th. The simple interval corresponding
to a 12th is a _____.

5th

---

13  A _____ corresponds to a 13th.

6th

---

14  For every compound general name there is a
corresponding _____ general name.

simple

---

15  Compound intervals are sometimes called by
the same general name as their corresponding
simple intervals. 14ths and larger intervals
are usually so called. A 14th is usually called
a(n) _____.

7th

---

16  10ths, 11ths, 12ths and 13ths
are occasionally called by
their corresponding simple
names. The given interval
might be called a _____
instead of a 12th.

5th

# Set 16 Minor scales

Write the B♭ harmonic minor scale. *(The locations of the DST's and aug 2nd may be marked first as a guide.)*

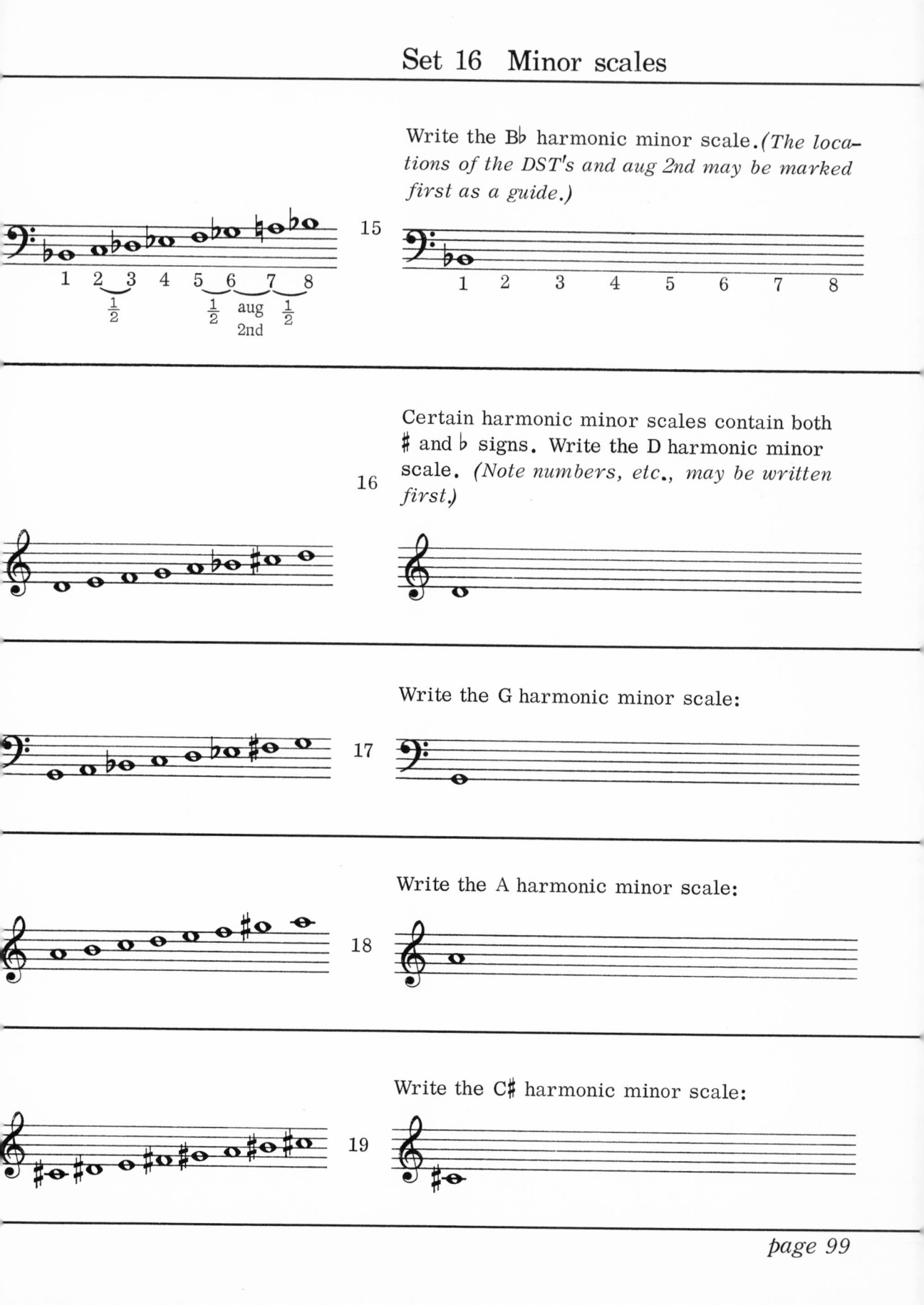

Certain harmonic minor scales contain both ♯ and ♭ signs. Write the D harmonic minor scale. *(Note numbers, etc., may be written first.)*

Write the G harmonic minor scale:

Write the A harmonic minor scale:

Write the C♯ harmonic minor scale:

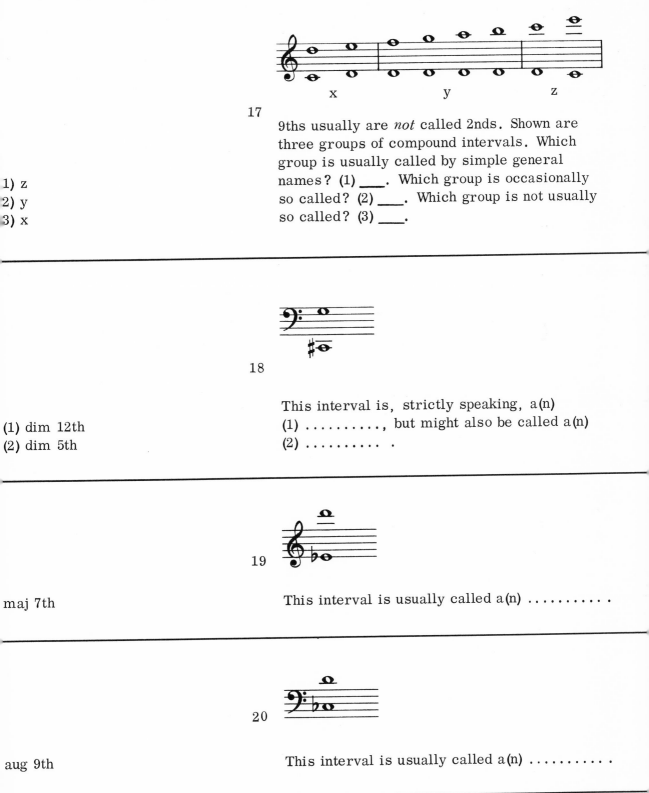

**17**

9ths usually are *not* called 2nds. Shown are
three groups of compound intervals. Which
group is usually called by simple general
names? (1) ___. Which group is occasionally
so called? (2) ___. Which group is not usually
so called? (3) ___.

1) z
2) y
3) x

**18**

This interval is, strictly speaking, a(n)
(1) .........., but might also be called a(n)
(2) .......... .

(1) dim 12th
(2) dim 5th

**19**

This interval is usually called a(n) .......... .

maj 7th

**20**

This interval is usually called a(n) .......... .

aug 9th

**10**

(1) DST
(2) aug 2nd
(3) DST

In the harmonic minor scale
5-6 is a(n) (1) .......... .
6-7 is a(n) (2) .......... .
7-8 is a(n) (3) .......... .

---

**11**

(1) 1   (2) 5
(3) 2-3

All forms of the minor scale, including the harmonic, have the same structure from note (1) ___ to note (2) ___, including a DST at (3) ___.

---

**12**

1-2 (whole tone)
2-3 DST
3-4 whole tone
4-5 whole tone
5-6 DST
6-7 aug 2nd
7-8 DST

Complete this structural description of the harmonic minor scale:

1-2 whole tone
2-3 .........
3-4 .........
4-5 .........
5-6 .........
6-7 .........
7-8 .........

---

**13**

Write the C harmonic minor scale. Mark the locations of the DST's and the aug 2nd first:

---

**14**

Because of the unusual nature of the aug 2nd, a sign should always be placed before note 7 in the harmonic minor scale. This is true even when the sign is a natural and technically unnecessary. Insert this sign in the F harmonic minor scale:

Construct a perf 11th above the given note.
*(Construct the corresponding simple interval;
then add an octave.)*

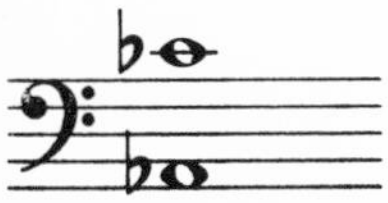

21

---

Construct a minor 10th below the given note:

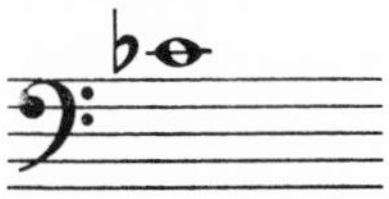

22

---

A

23   A major 10th above F is ___.

---

C♯

24   A perfect 12th below G♯ is ___.

---

D♯

25   A major 3rd above B is ___.

---

B

26   A diminished 7th below A♭ is ___.

---

perf 5th

27   G lies a . . . . . . . . . (what simple interval?)
above C.

---

min 7th

28   E♭ lies a . . . . . . . . . (what simple interval?)
below D♭.

---

unstable

29   A *consonant* interval is one which sounds
stable. The opposite of consonant is *dissonant*.
A dissonant interval sounds _____.

# Set 16  Minor scales

Write the first 5 notes of the F minor scale:

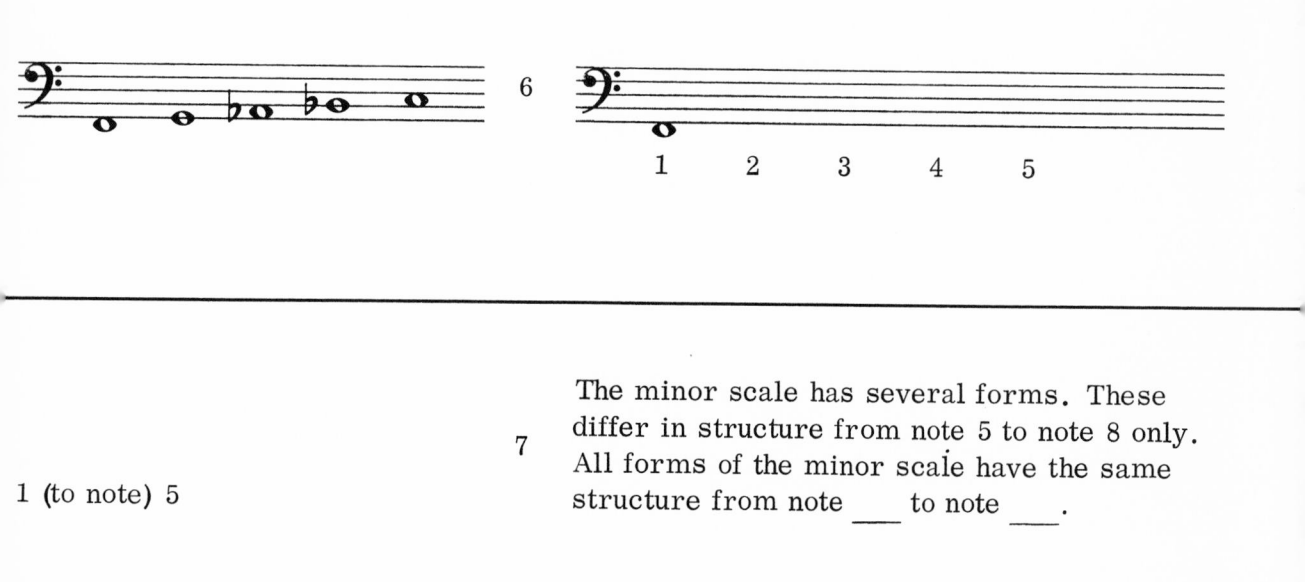

6

| 1 | 2 | 3 | 4 | 5 |

---

1 (to note) 5

7

The minor scale has several forms. These differ in structure from note 5 to note 8 only. All forms of the minor scale have the same structure from note ___ to note ___.

---

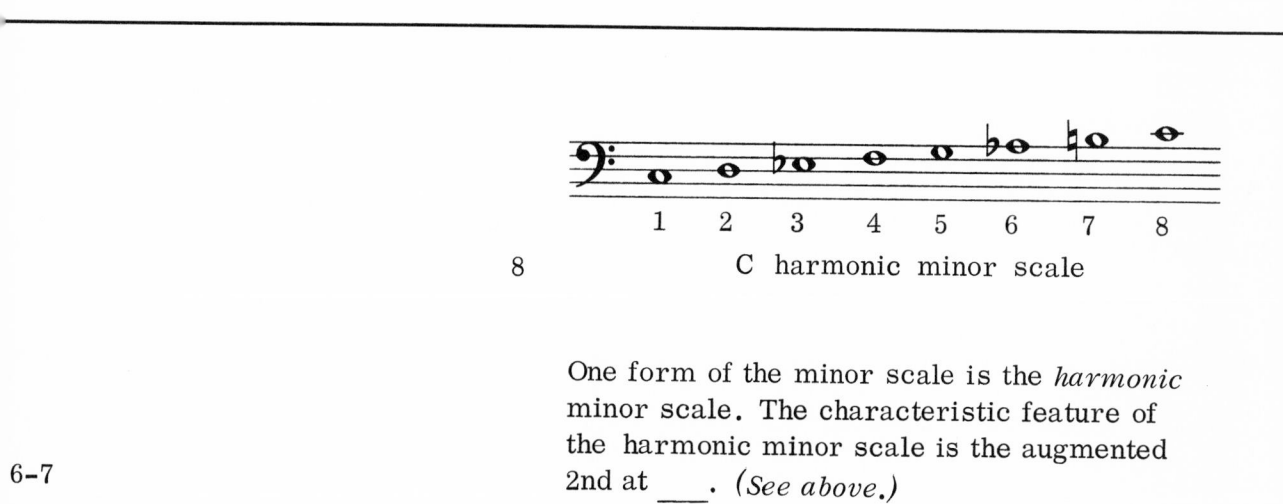

8

C harmonic minor scale

One form of the minor scale is the *harmonic* minor scale. The characteristic feature of the harmonic minor scale is the augmented 2nd at ___. *(See above.)*

6-7

---

(1) harmonic
(2) DST
(3) DST

9

The (1) _____ minor scale has an augmented 2nd at 6-7. 5-6 is a(n) (2) .......... . 7-8 is a(n) (3) .......... .

In traditional harmony the consonant intervals
are:

> all perfect intervals
> major and minor 3rds and 6ths

**30**

s    t    w    x    y    z

**(1) w (and) z  (2) consonant**

Intervals s, (1) ____ and ____, are (2) _____
intervals.

---

**31**  Intervals other than those listed above are
dissonant. Thus:

> all aug and dim intervals
> all 2nds and 7ths

**dissonant**

are _____ intervals.

---

One irregularity: The perfect 4th is consonant
only when accompanied by a note a 3rd lower
than its bottom note.

**32**

x    y

In case x the perf 4th GC
is (1) _____. In case y
the perf 4th GC is
(2) _____.

**(1) consonant**

**(2) dissonant**

---

**stable**

**33**  A consonant interval sounds _____.

---

w        x        y        z

**34**

Two intervals written differently but played
identically on the keyboard are *enharmonic
equivalents*. Interval w is the enharmonic

**z**

equivalent of interval ____.

# Set 16   Minor scales

**1**

(1) 3–4
(2) 7–8   (3) whole tones

The major scale has DST's at (1) ___ and (2) ___ and (3) ......... everywhere else.

**2**

2–3

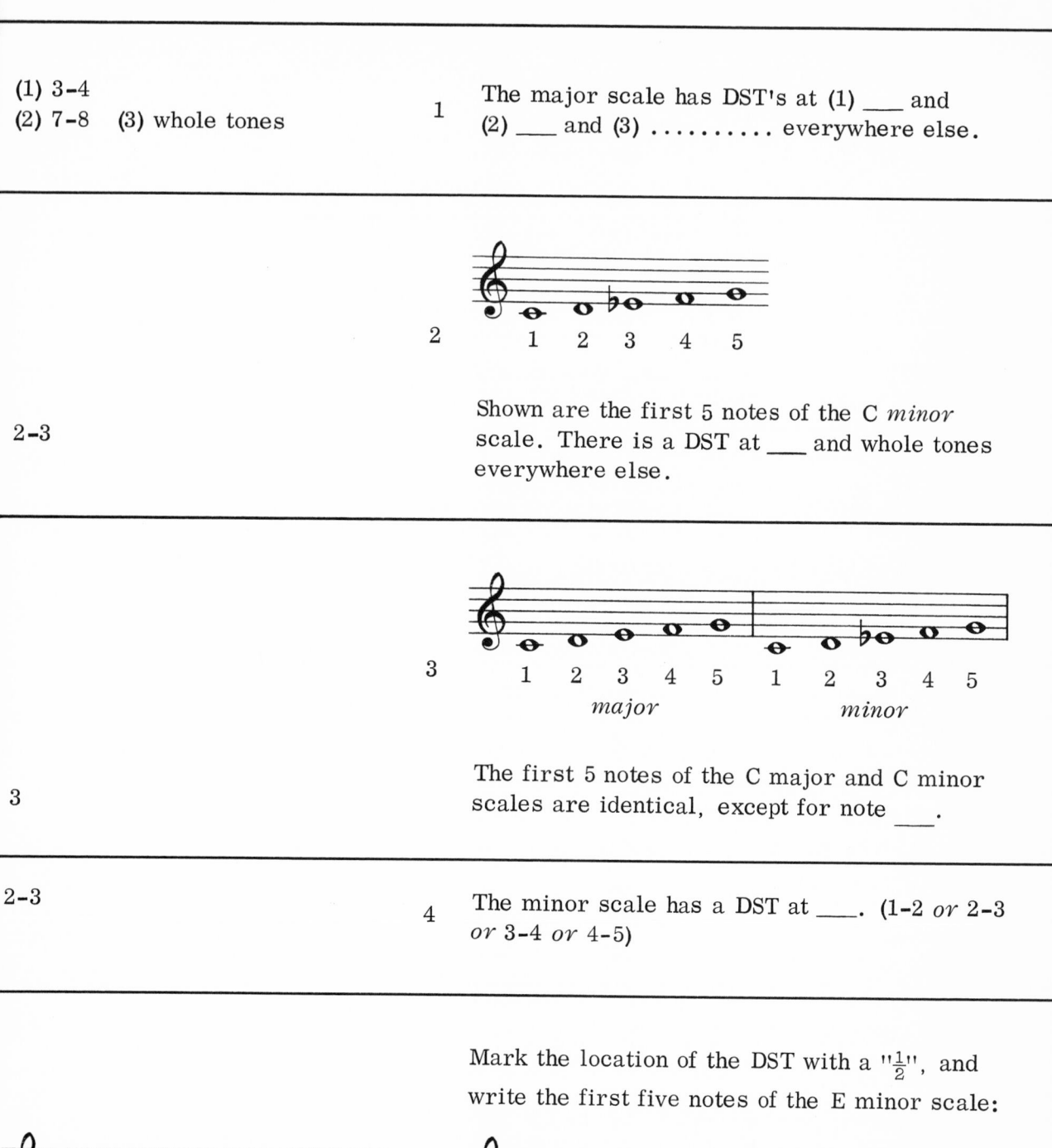

Shown are the first 5 notes of the C *minor* scale. There is a DST at ___ and whole tones everywhere else.

**3**

3

The first 5 notes of the C major and C minor scales are identical, except for note ___ .

**4**

2–3

The minor scale has a DST at ___ . (1-2 *or* 2-3 *or* 3-4 *or* 4-5)

**5**

Mark the location of the DST with a "½", and write the first five notes of the E minor scale:

| | | | |
|---|---|---|---|
| enharmonic equivalents | 35 | *(music notation)* | These two intervals are _____ _____. |

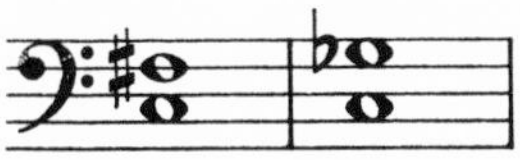

y

| | | |
|---|---|---|
| | 36 | *(music notation: w x y z)* A simple interval is *inverted* when its lower note is raised an octave, or when its upper note is lowered an octave. Interval ___ is an inversion of interval w. |

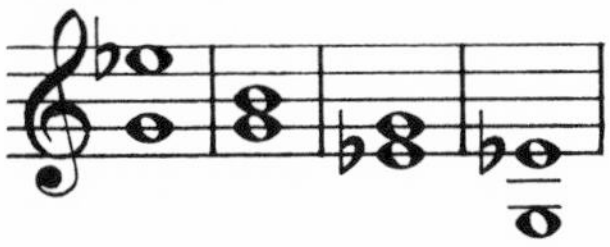

*(music notation)* or *(music notation)*

| | | | |
|---|---|---|---|
| | 37 | Invert: *(music notation)* | *(There are two possible correct answers.)* |

4th

| | | |
|---|---|---|
| | 38 | When the general name of an interval is subtracted from 9, the result is the general name of the inversion. Thus a 3rd becomes a 6th when inverted. A 5th becomes a _____ when inverted. |

major ⟷ minor
augmented ⟷ diminished
perfect ⟷ perfect

maj 2nd

| | | |
|---|---|---|
| | 39 | The above diagrams show the effect of inversion on specific interval names. Major intervals become minor and vice versa. Augmented intervals become diminished and vice versa. Perfect intervals remain perfect. A minor 7th becomes a (n) _____ _____ when inverted. |

dim 5th

| | | |
|---|---|---|
| | 40 | The inversion of an aug 4th is a(n) _____ _____ |

inversion

| | | |
|---|---|---|
| | 41 | *(music notation: x y)* Interval y is an _____ of interval x. |

Write the key signatures:

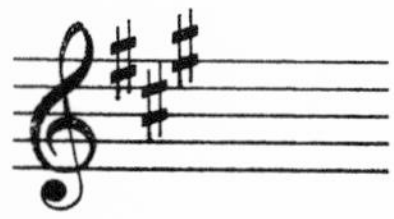

39   A major:

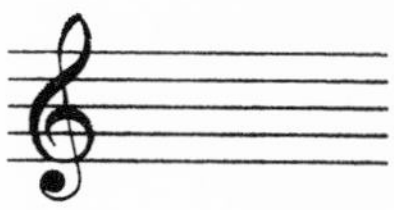

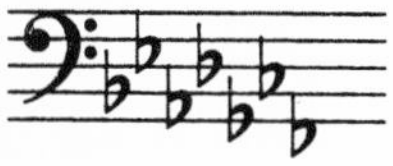

40   C♭ major:

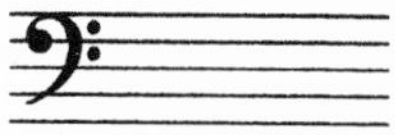

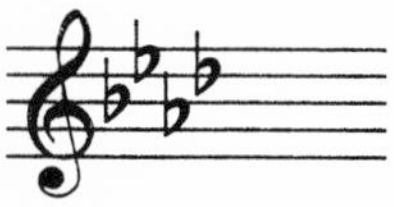

41   A♭ major:

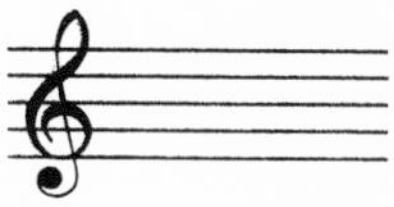

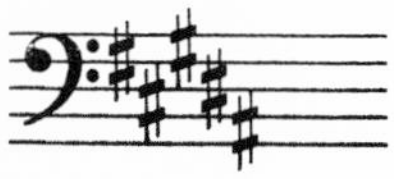

42   B major:

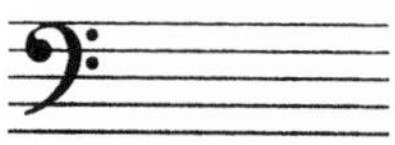

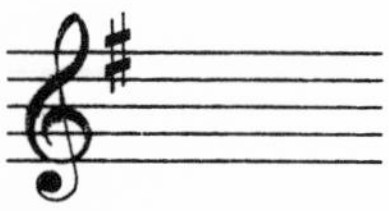

43   G major:

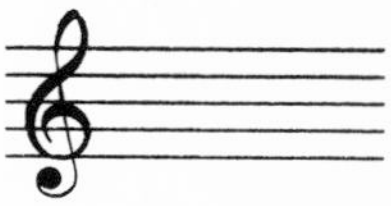

This set is a test covering parts 1 and 2. Its purpose is to show what material you need to review, if any. When you miss a question, make a note of the set number given with the answer and review that set after completing the test. If you omitted sets 10 and 11, omit frames 7, 9, 13, 19, 21, 23, 28, 35 and 36 in this set.

| | | |
|---|---|---|
| (1) transposed (2) does not  (Set 10) | 1 | When both notes of an interval are raised (or lowered) equally, the interval is said to be (1) _____. This operation (2) ......... (does *or* does not) change the size of the interval. |

2

dim 5th    (Set 9)

Name the interval: .........

| | | |
|---|---|---|
| prime (and) octave *(either order)*  (Set 5) | 3 | Most general names are ordinal numbers. The two exceptions are _____ and _____. |

| | | |
|---|---|---|
| G♭  (Set 3) | 4 | A whole tone below A♭ is \_\_\_. |

| | | |
|---|---|---|
| the relationship between two pitches  (Set 5) | 5 | An interval is ......... . |

Construct a perf 5th above the given note.

(Sets 8 and 9)

6

Name the major key corresponding to each
of the following signatures:

34

E

35

E♭

36

B♭

37

F♯

38

D♭

| | | |
|---|---|---|
| (1) 14th<br><br>(2) 9th<br>     (Set 11) | 7 | The general name (1) _____ and larger general names are usually reduced to simple general names. The general name (2)_____ is usually *not* reduced. General names falling between those two limits are occasionally reduced. |
| (Set 4) | 8 | Write the A♯ major scale: |
| transpose<br>    (Set 10) | 9 | When the major scale built on the lower note of an interval includes 𝙭's or ♭♭'s, it is convenient to _____ the interval in order to determine its name. |
| perf 4th<br>    (Set 9) | 10 | Name the interval: ......... |
| (1) double<br>(2) specific<br>(3) general<br>    (Set 6) | 11 | Every interval has a (1)_____ name, consisting of a (2) _____ name followed by a (3)_____ name. |
| (1) chromatic<br><br>(2) diatonic<br>    (Set 2) | 12 | In a (1) _____ semitone both notes are written on the same line or space. This is not true of a (2) _____ semitone. |

x        y

**(1) Ab**
**(2) Ab**

28   A different short-cut is used for the flat signatures. The tonic is the same as the next-to-the-last flat. The next-to-the-last flat of signature x is Eb. Therefore, the key is Eb major. The next-to-the-last flat of signature y is (1) ___. Therefore, the key is (2) ___ major.

**F**

29

For a signature of only one flat the short-cut does not work, but is hardly necessary.

One flat is the signature of ___ major.

**(1) higher (*or* upper)**
**(2) lower**
**(3) lower**
**(4) higher (*or* upper)**

30   If the tonics of two scales are a perfect 5th apart, the (1) _____ scale has one more sharp than the (2) _____ scale,  or the (3) _____ scale has one more flat than the (4) _____.

**(1) scale  (2) key signature**
  **(*either order*)**

31   The (1) ......... and the (2) ......... of a given major key have the same signs.

**(1) F♯**
**(2) Bb**

32   The first sharp is (1) ___.
The first flat is (2) ___.

**(1) ascending (*or* upward)**
**(2) descending (*or* downward)**

33   The order of sharps in a key signature is a series of (1) _____ 5ths.  The order of flats is a series of (2) _____ 5ths.

(1) simple

(2) compound

(Set 11)

13    Intervals with general names not greater than *octave* are (1) _____ intervals. Intervals with general names greater than *octave* are (2) _____ intervals.

---

G♯

(Sets 7 and 8)

14    ____ lies a minor 9th below A.

---

(Sets 8 and 9)

15    Construct a dim octave below the given note:

---

chromatic

(Set 2)

16    G and G♯ form a _____ semitone.

---

major 7th

(Set 7)

17    C𝄪 lies a ......... (what simple interval?) above D♯.

---

(Sets 7 and 8)

18    Construct an aug 6th above the given note:

---

(1) doubly aug

(2) doubly dim

(Set 10)

19    An interval one CST larger than an augmented interval has the specific name (1) ......... . An interval one CST smaller than a diminished interval has the specific name (2) ......... .

24

Questions in the form: "What key has x number of sharps (or flats)" may be answered by referring to the series of perfect 5ths up (or down) from C. We know that the key of B major has 5 sharps because B lies 5 perfect 5ths (1) _____ (above *or* below) (2)___ .

(1) above   (2) C

25

There is a short-cut method for finding major keys from a given signature. The tonic note always lies a DST above the last sharp. In this signature the last sharp is (1) ___. Therefore, the key is (2)___ major.

(1) G♯
(2) A

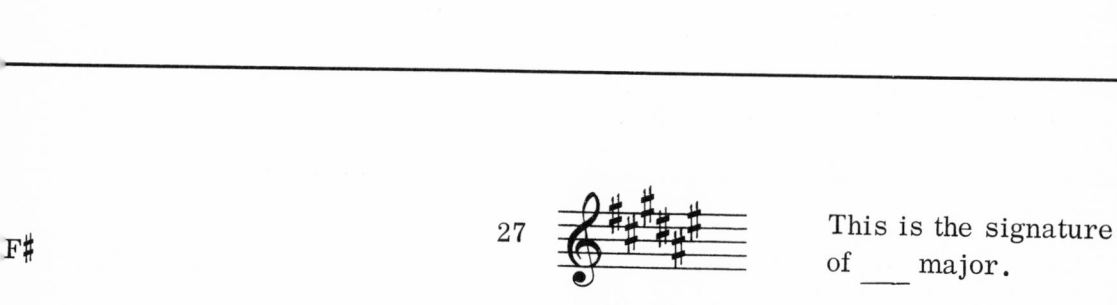

(1) C♯
(2) D

26

In this signature the last sharp is (1) ___, and the key is (2) ___ major.

F♯

27

This is the signature of ___ major.

whole tone
    (Set 3)

20   Two semitones make a _____  _____.

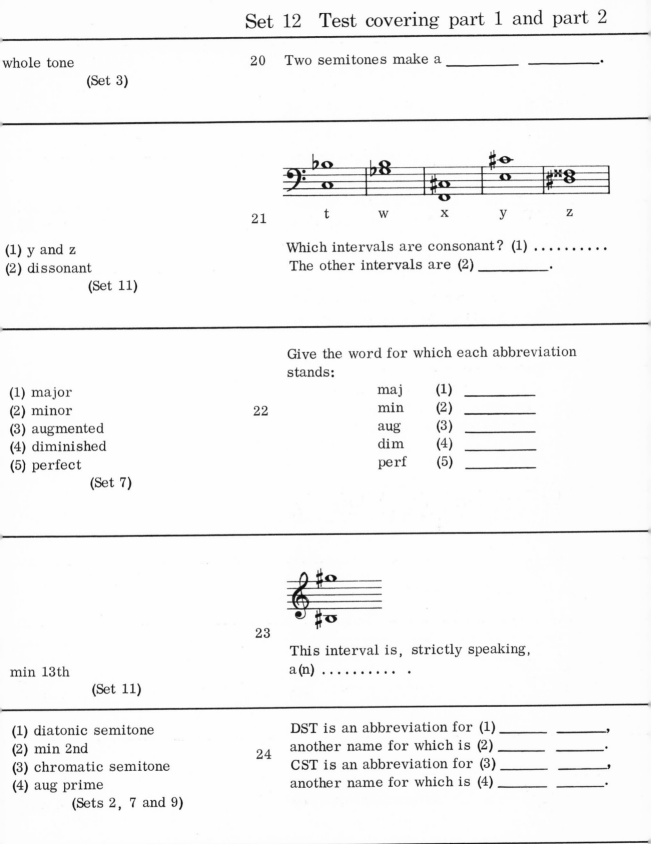

21   t   w   x   y   z

(1) y and z
(2) dissonant
    (Set 11)

Which intervals are consonant? (1) .........
The other intervals are (2) _____.

Give the word for which each abbreviation
stands:

(1) major
(2) minor
(3) augmented
(4) diminished
(5) perfect
    (Set 7)

22

| maj | (1) | _____ |
| min | (2) | _____ |
| aug | (3) | _____ |
| dim | (4) | _____ |
| perf | (5) | _____ |

23

min 13th
    (Set 11)

This interval is, strictly speaking,
a(n) .......... .

(1) diatonic semitone
(2) min 2nd
(3) chromatic semitone
(4) aug prime
    (Sets 2, 7 and 9)

24   DST is an abbreviation for (1) _____ _____,
another name for which is (2) _____ _____.
CST is an abbreviation for (3) _____ _____,
another name for which is (4) _____ _____.

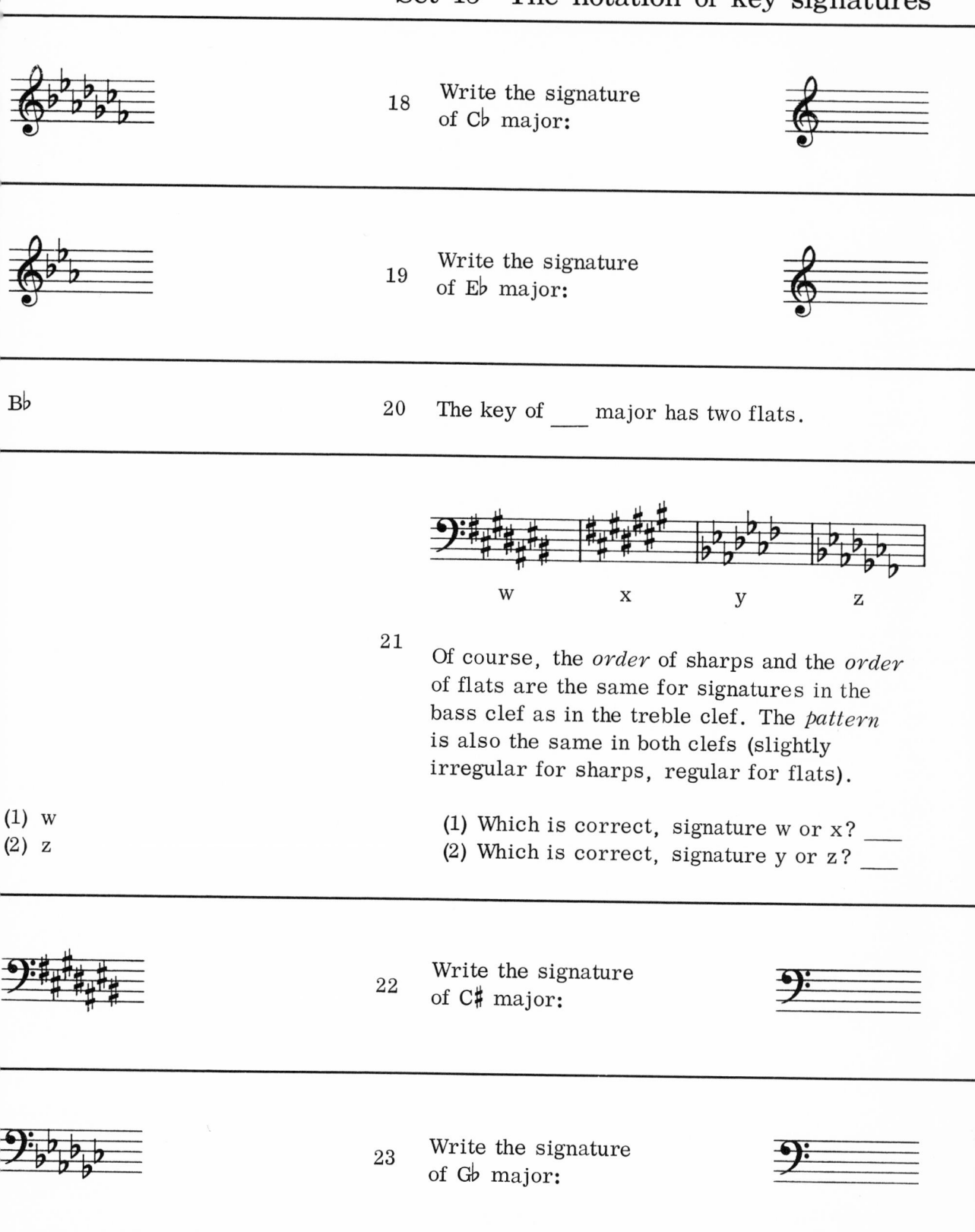

18   Write the signature
of Cb major:

19   Write the signature
of Eb major:

Bb

20   The key of ___ major has two flats.

w          x          y          z

21

Of course, the *order* of sharps and the *order*
of flats are the same for signatures in the
bass clef as in the treble clef. The *pattern*
is also the same in both clefs (slightly
irregular for sharps, regular for flats).

(1) w
(2) z

(1) Which is correct, signature w or x? ___
(2) Which is correct, signature y or z? ___

22   Write the signature
of C# major:

23   Write the signature
of Gb major:

B major scale
  (Set 4)

25   B  C♯  D♯  E  F♯  G♯  A♯  B spells the
.......... . *(Be specific.)*

---

(1) major

(2) perfect
  (Sets 6 and 9)

26   If (and only if) the upper note of the interval falls into the major scale built on the lower note, the specific name is (1) _____ in the case of 2nds, 3rds, 6ths and 7ths; and (2) (2) _____ in the case of primes, 4ths, 5ths and octaves.

---

Construct a min 3rd above the given note:

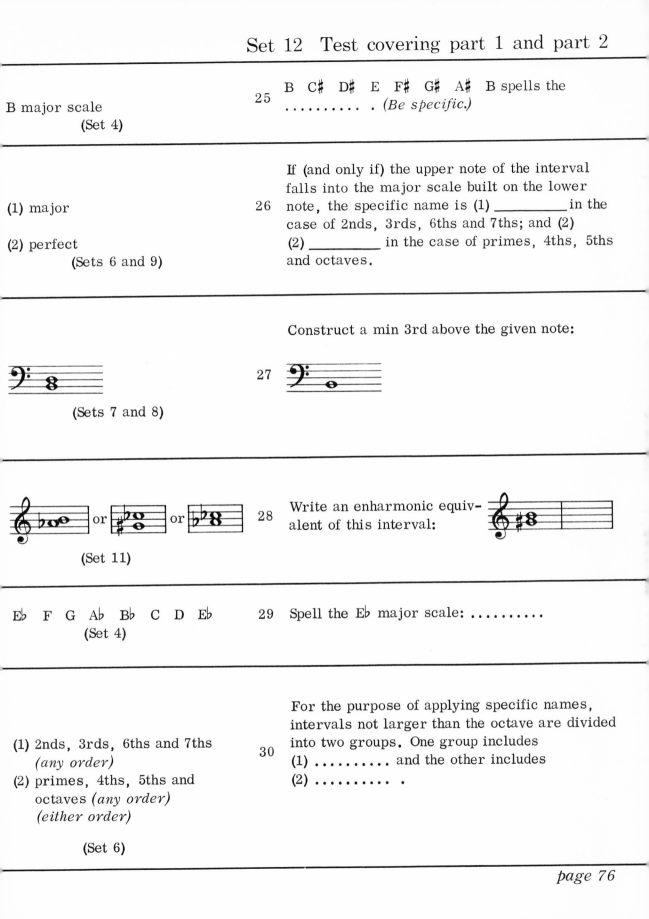

(Sets 7 and 8)

27

---

or  or

(Set 11)

28   Write an enharmonic equiv- alent of this interval:

---

E♭  F  G  A♭  B♭  C  D  E♭
  (Set 4)

29   Spell the E♭ major scale: .........

---

(1) 2nds, 3rds, 6ths and 7ths
    *(any order)*
(2) primes, 4ths, 5ths and
    octaves *(any order)*
    *(either order)*

    (Set 6)

30   For the purpose of applying specific names, intervals not larger than the octave are divided into two groups. One group includes (1) .......... and the other includes (2) .......... .

---

14

In the flat signatures, each flat lies a 5th lower (or a 4th higher) than the preceding flat. The third flat is A♭. The fourth flat is ___.

D♭

---

15

The order of flats in the key signatures is a series of *descending* fifths.   Complete this table:

| 1st♭ | 2nd♭ | 3rd♭ | 4th♭ | 5th♭ | 6th♭ | 7th♭ |
|---|---|---|---|---|---|---|
| — | — | A♭ | D♭ | — | — | — |

B♭  E♭  (A♭  D♭)  G♭  C♭  F♭

---

16

The key with one flat is (1) ___ major.
The first flat is (2) ___.

(1) F

(2) B♭

---

17

Copy the given signature in the extra space:

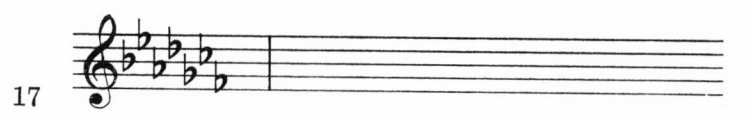

In the flat signatures, flats ......... (are *or* are not) placed on the staff in a regular up-down pattern.

are

| | | |
|---|---|---|
| (1) dim min maj aug<br><br>(2) dim perf aug<br>(Sets 7 and 9) | 31 | List these terms — min, aug, maj, dim — in order, from smallest to largest:<br>(1) _____ _____ _____ _____.<br>List these terms —perf, dim, aug— in the same way: (2)_____ _____ _____. |
| (1) adjacent<br>(2) semitone (*or* CST)<br>(Set 1) | 32 | These two notes are played on (1) _____ keys. The notes are one (2) _____ apart. |
| maj 2nd (*or* whole tone)<br>(Set 6) | 33 | Name the interval: ......... |
| z<br>(Set 4) | 34 | Which of the scales, if any, are major scales? ......... |
| simple<br>(Set 11) | 35 | The specific name of a compound interval is the same as the specific name of the corresponding _____ interval. |
| minor 3rd<br>(Set 11) | 36 | The inversion of a major 6th is a(n) _____ _____. |

Copy the signature and add three more sharps making a total of 7 sharps:

10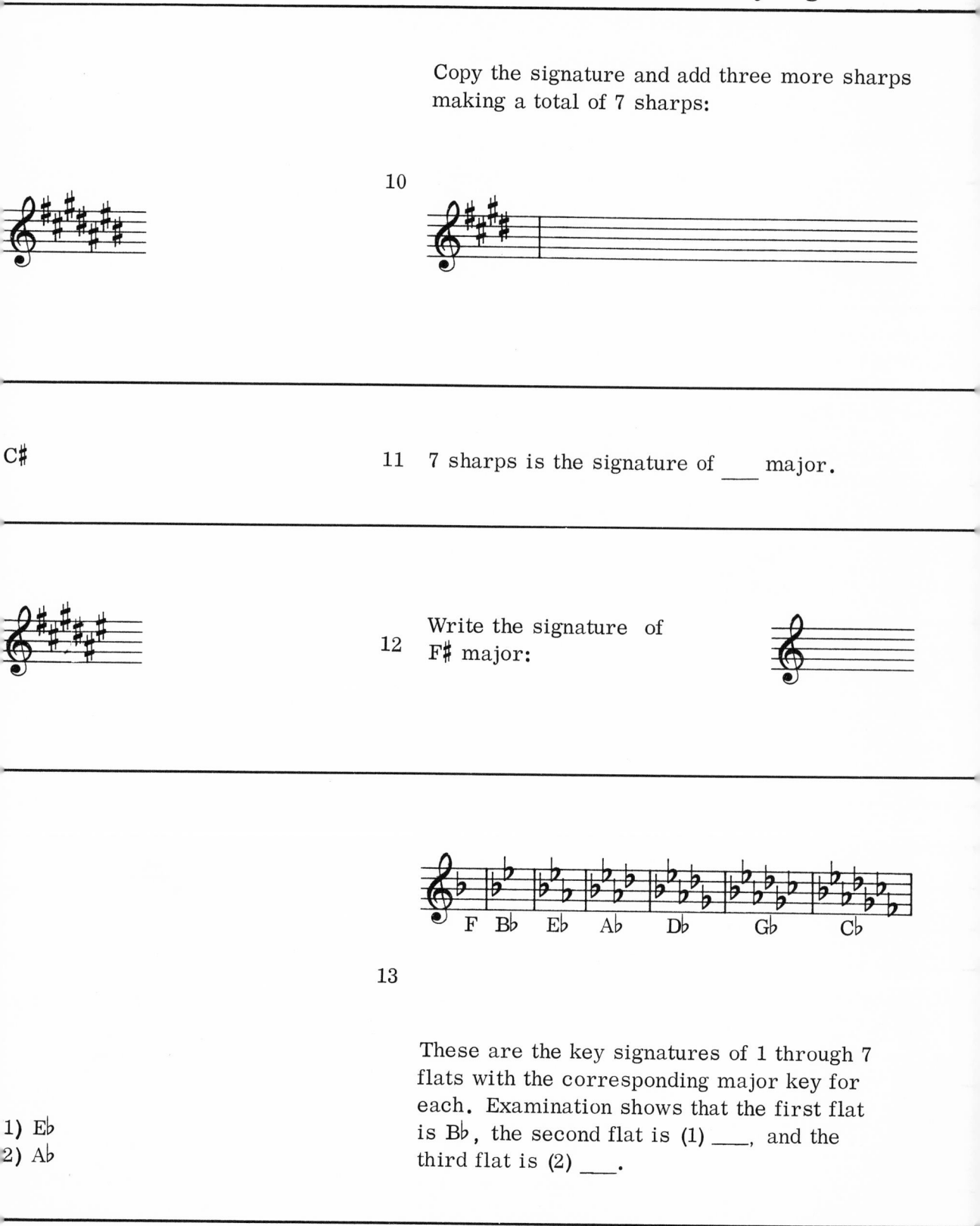

C♯

11   7 sharps is the signature of ___ major.

12   Write the signature of F♯ major:

F   B♭   E♭   A♭   D♭   G♭   C♭

13

1) E♭

2) A♭

These are the key signatures of 1 through 7 flats with the corresponding major key for each. Examination shows that the first flat is B♭, the second flat is (1) ___, and the third flat is (2) ___.

# PART 3 KEY SIGNATURES
# THE MINOR SCALES
## Set 13 The series of 5ths

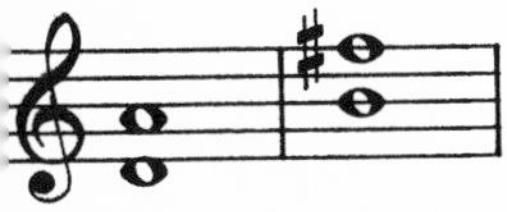

1 Construct a perfect 5th above each of the following notes:

2 Construct a perfect 5th below each of the following notes:

E

3 A perfect 5th above A is ___.

D♭

4 A perfect 5th above G♭ is ___.

B♭

5 A perfect 5th below F is ___.

F♯

6 A perfect 5th below C♯ is ___.

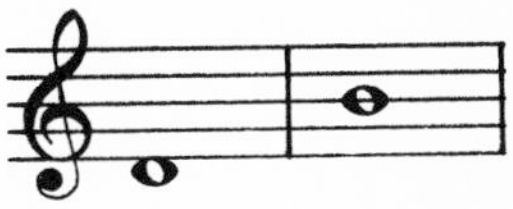

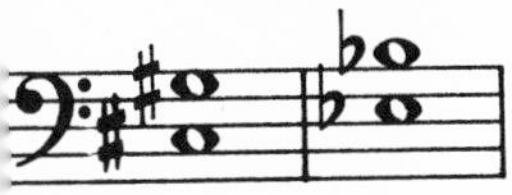

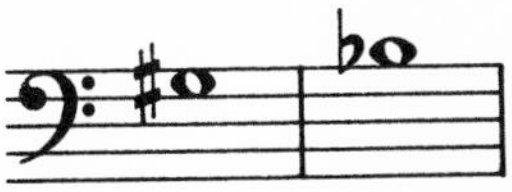

A

7 C G D ?

Shown above is a series of perfect 5ths beginning on C. G is a perfect 5th higher than C; D is a perfect 5th higher than G. What is the next higher member of the series? ___

(C G D A) E B F♯ (C♯)

8 Fill in the three missing members of this series:

C G D A _ _ _ C♯

E♭

9 ? B♭ F C

Above is another series of perfect 5ths. It proceeds *down* from C. F is a perfect 5th lower than C. B♭ is a perfect 5th lower than F. What is the next member of the series? ___

(C♭) G♭ D♭ A♭ (E♭ B♭ F C)

10 Fill in the three missing members of this series:

C♭ _ _ _ E♭ B♭ F C

perf 5th

11 C♭ G♭ D♭ A♭ E♭ B♭ F C G D A E B F♯ C♯

This series is a combination of the series above C and the series below C. Each member of the series is a ________ ________ higher than the next lower member.

5 The order of sharps in the key signatures is a series of ascending 5ths. Complete this table:

(F♯ C♯) G♯ D♯ A♯ E♯ B♯

| 1st♯ | 2nd♯ | 3rd♯ | 4th♯ | 5th♯ | 6th♯ | 7th♯ |
|------|------|------|------|------|------|------|
| F♯ | C♯ | __ | __ | __ | __ | __ |

(1) C

(2) G

(3) F♯

6 The key with no sharps or flats is (1) ___ major.
The key with one sharp is (2) ___ major.
The first sharp is (3) ___ .

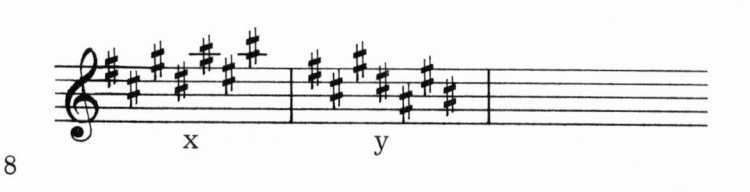

x        y        z

7 In "signature" x the order of sharps is correct (F♯, C♯, G♯). The signature looks strange because the first sharp should be written an octave higher, as in signature y. In signature z the last sharp should be written . . . . . . . . . . .

an octave lower

x        y

8 Signature x has a regular down-up pattern, but requires ledger lines. Signature y has a slightly irregular pattern, but avoids ledger lines. Which is correct? ___

y

- 

9 Copy signature y in the space provided above.

Fill in the missing members of this series of perfect 5ths:

♭b  G♭  D♭  (A♭)  E♭  B♭  F     **12**

\_\_ \_\_ \_\_ A♭ \_\_ \_\_ \_\_ C \_\_ \_\_ \_\_

C)  G  D  A  (E)  B  F♯  C♯

E \_\_ \_\_ \_\_

---

**13**

1) D major     Scale x is the (1) \_\_ _____ scale.

2) A major     Scale y is the (2) \_\_ _____ scale.

---

(1) 5

(2) perf 5th     **14**

In frame 13 the arrow shows that scale y is built on note (1) \_\_\_ *(what number?)* of scale x. The interval between the two tonics is a (2) _____ _____.

---

**15**

Examination shows that the D major scale contains the same notes as the A major scale with one exception: The D major scale contains G (1) \_\_\_ (♭, ♮ *or* ♯), while the A major scale contains G (2) \_\_\_.

(1) ♮

(2) ♯

---

**16**

(1) A(♮)

(2) A♯

These two scales have tonics a perfect 5th apart. Again there is one point of difference in the scales' content: The E major scale contains (1) \_\_\_ *(name of note)* while the B major scale contains (2) \_\_\_.

1

The signs in a key signature are always written in the same order. The key signature of
E major is written as in ___ (x *or* y).

x

These are the key signatures of 1 through 7
sharps, and the major key corresponding to
each signature. In all the signatures the first
sharp is F♯. In those having two or more
sharps, the second sharp is C♯. In those having three or more sharps, the third sharp is

___ .

2

3   The first sharp is ___ .

In the sharp signatures, each sharp lies a
5th higher (or a 4th lower) than the preceding
sharp. Since the first sharp is F♯, the second
sharp is ___ .

4

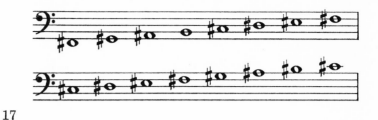

17

When the tonics of two scales lie a perfect 5th
apart, the higher scale will have one more
sharp than the lower scale. The example above
shows that the (1) ___ _____ scale has
one more sharp than the (2) ___ _____
scale.

(1) C♯ major

(2) F♯ major

18

In counting the number of signs in a scale the
same note name is not counted twice. In the
C♯ major scale, C♯ is counted only once. The
C♯ major scale has ___ sharps.

7

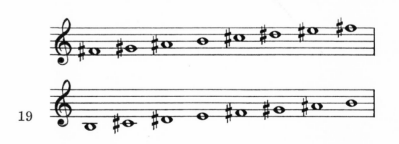

19

The F♯ major scale has ___ more sharp(s)
than the B major scale.

one

When the tonics of two scales lie a perfect 5th
20  apart, the higher scale will have ___ _____
sharp(s) than the lower scale.

one more

20

Major key signatures can also be found by scale contruction. The F♯ major scale, containing (1) ___ sharps, shows that the signature of F♯ major is (2) ___ sharps.

1) 6

2) 6

---

Write the C♭ major scale:

21

flats

This shows that the signature of C♭ major is __ _____.

---

22

Find the signatures of the following keys, using either the series of 5ths or scale construction:

(1) A major: ___ _____
(2) C♯ major: ___ _____

1) 3 sharps

2) 7 sharps

---

23

To find the major key when the signature is known, count up (for sharps) or down (for flats) from C in the series of 5ths.

What major key has a signature of 4 sharps? __

(4 perf 5ths above C.)

---

24 What major key has a signature of 5 flats? __

)♭

---

25 5 sharps is the signature of __ major.

---

26 What is the signature of A♭ major? __ _____

flats

---

27 What major key has a signature of 2 sharps? __

---

C  G  D  A  E  B  F♯  C♯

**21**   Each member of this series is a _____
_____ higher than the next lower member.

perf 5th

---

**22**   Suppose that the notes in the above series represent the tonics of scales. Each note is a perfect 5th higher than the note to its left and represents a scale having _____
_____ _____ than the note to its left.

one more
sharp

---

*(Refer to the above series (frame 21) for the next two frames.)*

**23**   The E major scale has _____ _____
_____ than the A major scale.

one more
sharp

---

**24**   The E major scale has _____ _____
_____ than the D major scale.

two more
sharps

---

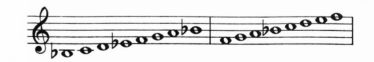

**25**   The tonics of these two scales lie a
(1) ..........apart. The *lower* scale has
(2) _____ _____ flat(s) than the *upper* scale.

(1) perf 5th
(2) one more

---

**26**   The tonics in these scales are a(n) (1) ..........
apart. The lower scale has (2) _____
_____ flat(s) than the upper scale.

(1) perf 5th
(2) one more
   *(The note B♭ is counted only once in the B♭ scale.)*

# Set 14   Major key signatures

Tell whether each key is a "sharp" key or a "flat" key:

**11**

(1) sharp    C♯ major is a (1) _____ key.
(2) flat     A♭ major is a (2) _____ key.
(3) flat     F  major is a (3) _____ key.
(4) sharp    D  major is a (4) _____ key.

**12**

(1) F        With the exception of C major and (1) ___ major, all major keys without "flat" or

(2) sharp    "sharp" in their names are (2) _____ keys.

**13**

Since D major is a *sharp* key its signature can be found by going *up* the series of fifths from

(1) 2        C. D lies (1) ___ *(how many?)* perfect fifths above C. Therefore, the signature of D major

(2) 2 sharps is (2) ___ _____.

**14**

(1) flat     E♭ major is a (1) _____ key. Therefore
(2) down     its signature is found by going (2) _____
             the series of 5ths from C. The signature of
(3) 3 flats  E♭ major is (3) ___ _____.

**15**     Give the signatures of the following keys:

5 sharps       B major ___ _____.

**16**

1 flat         F major ___ _____.

**17**

1 sharp        G major ___ _____.

**18**

6 flats        G♭ major ___ _____.

**19**

2 flats        B♭ major ___ _____.

| | | |
|---|---|---|
| (1) lower | 27 | When the tonics of two major scales in flats lie a perfect 5th apart, the (1) _____ (higher *or* lower) scale will have one more flat than the (2) _____ scale. |
| (2) higher | | |

| | | |
|---|---|---|
| one more flat | 28 | Cb  Gb  Db  Ab  Eb  Bb  F  C<br><br>Suppose that these notes represent the tonics of scales. Each note is a perfect 5th lower than the note to its right and represents a scale having _____  _____  _____ than the note to its right. |

| | | |
|---|---|---|
| one more flat | 29 | *(Refer to the above series for the next two frames.)*<br>The Db major scale has _____  _____  _____ than the Ab major scale. |

| | | |
|---|---|---|
| three more flats | 30 | The Gb major scale has _____  _____  _____ than the Eb major scale. |

| | | |
|---|---|---|
| (1) sharp<br>(2) flat | 31 | These relationships are easily remembered by associating *sharp* with *high*, and *flat* with *low*. Thus, if the tonics of two scales lie a perfect 5th apart, the higher scale has one more (1) _____, or the lower scale has one more (2) _____. |

| | | |
|---|---|---|
| 7  6  5  (4)  3  2  (1 no 1)<br>2  3  (4)  5  6  7 | 32 | Since the C major scale has no sharps or flats, the G major scale has one sharp and the F major scale has one flat. Fill in the blanks in the following chart:<br><br>Cb Gb Db Ab Eb Bb  F  C  G  D  A  E  B  F# C#<br>__ __ __ 4 __ __  1 no 1 __ __ 4 __ __ __<br>           flats       #'s     sharps<br>                        or<br>                        b's |

| | | |
|---|---|---|
| Cb  Gb  Db  Ab  Eb  Bb  F  (C)<br>G  D  A  E  B  F#  C# | 33 | Fill in the blanks:<br><br>                                   C<br>__ __ __ __ __ __ __  no  __ __ __ __ __ __ __<br>7  6  5  4  3  2  1      1  2  3  4  5  6  7<br>        flats            #'s       sharps<br>                          or<br>                          b's |

# Set 14   Major key signatures

| C♭ | G♭ | D♭ | A♭ | E♭ | B♭ | F | C | G | D | A | E | B | F♯ | C♯ |
|----|----|----|----|----|----|----|----|----|----|----|----|----|----|----|
| 7  | 6  | 5  | 4  | 3  | 2  | 1  | no | 1 | 2 | 3 | 4 | 5 | 6  | 7  |

flats         ♯'s      sharps
or
♭'s

**6**

This chart shows not only the signs for each major *scale*, but also the signs for each

. . . . . . . . . . .

(major key)
signature

---

*(Refer to the above chart for frames 7, 8, 9 and 10.)*

**7**

no
sharps (or) flats

The key signature of C major is ___

_____ or _____.

---

4
sharps

**8**   The key signature of E major is ___

_____.

---

(1) flat
(2) sharp
(3) flat   (4) sharp

**9**   Keys having one or more sharps in the signature are called "sharp keys." Keys having one or more flats in the signature are called "flat keys." D♭ major is a (1)_____ key. F♯ major is a (2) _____ key.  F major is a (3) _____ key.  A major is a (4) _____ key.

---

F

**10**   The only "flat" major key without "flat" in its name (as in B♭, E♭, etc.) is ___ major.

key

1    A piece in the <u>k</u>_____ of F major ordinarily uses the F major scale.

D♭ major scale

2    A piece in the key of D♭ major ordinarily uses the ___ _____ _____.

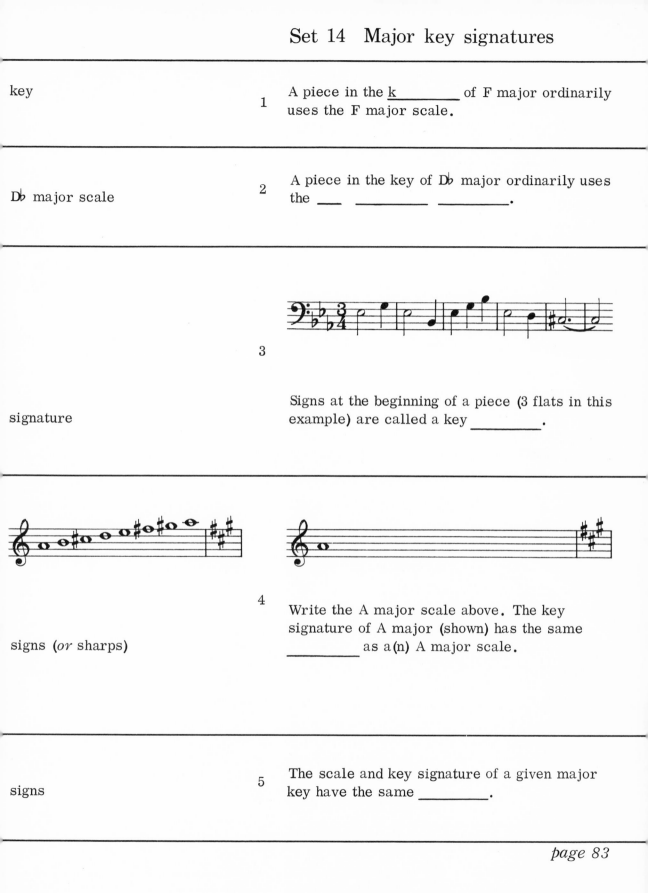

3

signature

Signs at the beginning of a piece (3 flats in this example) are called a key _____.

4

signs (*or* sharps)

Write the A major scale above. The key signature of A major (shown) has the same _____ as a(n) A major scale.

signs

5    The scale and key signature of a given major key have the same _____.